THE
INDISPENSABLE
EMPLOYEE

THE INDISPENSABLE EMPLOYEE

How to Keep Your Job in Hard Times

ERIC WEBER

BERKLEY BOOKS, NEW YORK

THE BERKLEY PUBLISHING GROUP
Published by the Penguin Group
Penguin Group (USA) Inc.
375 Hudson Street, New York, New York 10014, USA
Penguin Group (Canada), 90 Eglinton Avenue East, Suite 700, Toronto, Ontario M4P 2Y3, Canada
(a division of Pearson Penguin Canada Inc.)
Penguin Books Ltd., 80 Strand, London WC2R 0RL, England
Penguin Group Ireland, 25 St. Stephen's Green, Dublin 2, Ireland (a division of Penguin Books Ltd.)
Penguin Group (Australia), 250 Camberwell Road, Camberwell, Victoria 3124, Australia
(a division of Pearson Australia Group Pty. Ltd.)
Penguin Books India Pvt. Ltd., 11 Community Centre, Panchsheel Park, New Delhi—110 017, India
Penguin Group (NZ), 67 Apollo Drive, Rosedale, North Shore 0632, New Zealand
(a division of Pearson New Zealand Ltd.)
Penguin Books (South Africa) (Pty.) Ltd., 24 Sturdee Avenue, Rosebank, Johannesburg 2196,
South Africa

Penguin Books Ltd., Registered Offices: 80 Strand, London WC2R 0RL, England

The publisher does not have any control over and does not assume responsibility for author or third-
party websites or their content.

PRINTING HISTORY
Berkley mass-market edition / April 1991
Revised Berkley trade paperback edition / June 2009

Library of Congress Cataloging-in-Publication Data

Weber, Eric, (date)
    The indispensable employee / Eric Weber.—Rev. Berkley trade pbk. ed.
        p.   cm.
    ISBN 978-0-425-23141-8
    1. Employees—Rating of. 2. Performance. 3. Time management. 4. Career development. I. Title.

    HF5549.5.R3W43   2009
    650.1—dc22   2009004656

PRINTED IN THE UNITED STATES OF AMERICA

10   9   8   7   6   5   4   3   2   1

Contents

Time Management

Making Yourself "Recession-Proof"

CONTENTS

Preface

I'm not sure you would have liked me very much back in the early stages of my career.

I had long hair, to my shoulders. I wore bush jeans and form-fitting polo shirts to work, even though I was a senior copywriter at a blue-chip advertising agency, earning today's equivalent of approximately two hundred fifty thousand dollars a year.

I had written a book in my spare time that had become a bestseller, receiving sustained publicity. I wrote another book, got a healthy advance on it, and went out and fulfilled a life-long ambition: I bought a forest-green/cream–colored 1949 Silver Wraith Rolls-Royce with a sunroof (that leaked horrendously, even in a drizzle) and right-hand drive.

So there I was; I thought I had it all—a sort of hippie wannabe in an outlandish car, driving around Manhattan as if I owned the place.

No, I don't think you would have liked me very much back in the day.

Neither, apparently, did the man who ran my department. Bonus time was nearing, and I'd had a good year, creating a couple of well-known and award-winning commercials. I was expecting something big.

My copy chief called me into his office, shook my hand perfunctorily, and handed me an envelope. I raced back to my office and ripped it open. What the—? There must be a zero missing, I thought. Definitely had to be a typo. It was about a tenth of what I'd expected. And I was outraged.

Nevertheless, I held my fire. I didn't want to act precipitously. I scheduled five minutes with my boss, Lenny, at the end of the day.

As I went through meetings and work sessions, I let my anger build slowly, evenly, mentally noting all the successes I'd had during the year. I was "injustice collecting" like crazy.

The appointed hour finally rolled around, and Lenny's secretary motioned for me to enter his office. I'll never forget it as long as I live. He stood behind his desk, his tie knot loosened, his stance combative, street-ready, his eyes on a sheaf of papers before him. "Yeah?" he said. He didn't indicate that I should sit. He didn't even look up.

"Listen, Lenny," I said. "I was kind of surprised at how small my bonus was. I thought I'd had a pretty good year."

He looked up slowly, snorted contemptuously, his mouth set in a sneer. He didn't say anything for what seemed like a decade, just looked me up and down like a fighter measuring his pathetic excuse for an opponent. Finally, he spoke. "You make me sick, Weber. You don't even deserve what you got. You think you're hot stuff, don't you, cruising around here like you're God's gift to advertising. I've seen a million guys like you. You write a few sweet commercials on the easy accounts, but when there's a crisis, I can't find you.

"You didn't want to work on the United Standard pitch because you don't like their corporate policies.

"You couldn't work on this because you were too busy. You didn't want to work on that because you don't have a feel for packaged goods." He stopped for a moment, the contempt in his eyes palpable. "You don't care about this company. You just care about yourself. Now get outta here."

Dumbstruck, I made a beeline for my office and shut the door. I sank to my knees, literally, my eyes welling with tears, a mixture of rage and mortification flushing my entire being. I didn't know whether to go back in there and take a swing at the man or beg his forgiveness. In the end, although I never have, I should have thanked him. It was one of those mon-umentally shocking and painful awakenings that you look back on years later and realize it actually redirected your life, dramatically, for the better.

I can't recall whether it took an hour, a day, or a week, but I know it wasn't long before I decided that I was going to show him that I *did* care about the company. (It is, in fact, the best company I'd ever worked for.) And if it took a whole new sense of rededication, of commitment, to prove it to Lenny, then I would take everything he could throw at me. And when I'd finished that, I would come back and ask him for more. No matter how overloaded, overworked, or overstressed I was, I would put the company first and myself second, and I would never whine, whimper, or complain. I would give my job my all and not even muse over what my bonus might or ought to be. I would leave it to my supervisors to decide.

And you know something?

I did.

And it was only then when my bonus started to meet and even exceed my expectations.

I've approached my job, whatever it is, with the same sense of dedication and commitment ever since. The satis-faction you derive from truly throwing yourself into the task at hand—instead of trying to get away with as little work as possible—is downright addictive.

A job well done *is* its own best reward. And it's what separates the few indispensable employees from the (army of) paper pushers.

You'll see.

What the Bosses Say

I interviewed top executives at ten successful companies to find out what they feel makes an employee indispensable. I figured that somewhere along the line in their outstanding careers, they would have come across one or two or maybe even a dozen people among the hundreds—and in some cases thousands—who've worked for them who had that special "something" that made their bosses feel that they were simply irreplaceable. My goal was to get to the heart of it—to understand "indispensableness"—so that I could communicate it to you and make you realize that it's not just about talent and brains.

So without further ado, let me describe our top ten execs.

The first, actually, is my brother Joe, who did a spectacular job building a medium-sized food company into a large one and who now owns a radio station in Atlanta. Then there are two—one a man, one a woman—who run global advertising mega-agencies. Another executive is the head of America's largest luxury leather goods concern, and another is the sales manager of a commercial real estate partnership. Next is a CFO of a giant packaged goods company, and another is COO of a children's clothing business. Two others run law firms, and the last boss is me. I used to be the executive creative director of a large New York City ad agency; now I run a company that makes independent movies.

Here are the questions I asked them (and myself): What are they looking for in their employees? What factors influence them to promote someone, while passing others by? How can an employee demonstrate that he is executive material? And what can an employee do to keep from getting fired when the numbers guy comes down the hall and tells your boss she's got to trim her payroll by, let's say, 28 percent?

This book is built around their answers—and, of course, around my own experience as a boss. I'm convinced you'll find it not only fascinating but incredibly helpful. There are dozens of things you can start doing right now to succeed—things that are sound business practice in a good economy, and are absolutely essential for success in a shaky one.

Read carefully. Put these suggestions to work. Experience the satisfaction that comes from knowing you're making the most of your talents and your opportunities. You'll discover along the way that, like almost every success in life, becoming an indispensable employee requires 10 percent inspiration and 90 percent perspiration.

Attitude
Adjustment

Chapter One

Reframing How You Think about Work

The early chapters of this book are going to discuss atti-
tudes about work. After that, we're going to concentrate
on the very tangible, practical steps you can take that will
make you someone who's pretty much "fire-proof."

The reason I want to discuss attitude first is because if you
can make a breakthrough in this area you can conquer the
world. If you can't, then all the practical advice we get to in
the later chapters will be virtually useless.

If you currently view your job as nothing more than a
job, something you do five days a week so you have enough
money to live, then that's a problem.

If you want to spend as little time as possible each day in
your place of business, that's a problem.

If you hate what you do, that's a problem.

If you plan on quitting as soon as the time is right, that's a problem.

If you don't like the company you work for or the people you work with, that's a problem.

If your attitude about work is that it will always be a waste of time, an onerous chore that keeps you from doing what you really want to do, that's a problem.

If any of the above describes you, you and I are on a totally different page. *I love work!* It has been my salvation. I was the laziest college student you've ever met in your life. Must have had attention deficit disorder. Probably should have been on cartloads of Ritalin. They just didn't diagnose it in those days. So I was sure that when I got out of school I was going to be an abject and dismal failure. After all, how was I going to survive at work—I simply couldn't concentrate. Got a job for $85 a week writing direct mail letters for three of Prentice Hall's book clubs. Unlike at school, I found I could concentrate more than fifteen minutes at a time. Sometimes I actually found myself staying late because I was almost enjoying perfecting a paragraph or two.

My boss would occasionally say "Good job." After four months I got a raise. I was shocked because I thought they were calling me in to fire me. Six months later I got another raise. It was awesome. Brimming with confidence, I applied for a job with a great NYC ad agency—Young & Rubicam. Miraculously, they hired me for considerably more than I'd previously been making. For the first time in my life I had a couple of bucks in my pocket. I moved into New York City, got a nice apartment. I could afford to take a date out to dinner at a decent restaurant.

Still, I had a bad attitude. It was work. The office. A place that got in the way of all the other things I wanted to do. Although what those things were, I've never been actually sure.

Nevertheless, the economy was on an upswing. I was pretty good at what I did. The raises kept on coming. Everything was all right with the world—until I got the jolt from my supervisor described in the introduction to this book.

What a blow! I was accused of not giving a damn about the company that was paying my salary. And here I thought I was God's gift to the place. It forced me to rethink everything.

I took stock. I had my own office, a pretty decent pension plan, and inexpensive health insurance. I had a secretary—shared with three other people, but nevertheless someone who answered my phone and filed my expense reports. (Holy cow, I even had an expense account!) I had a wonderful group of coworkers—many of whom had become good friends—I wrote television commercials seen by millions of people, worked with actors, models, great photographers. It suddenly occurred to me that I was the most selfish person on the face of the earth. Young & Rubicam, the ad agency for whom I was working at the time, was one of the warmest, most generous companies in the world. What the hell was the matter with me? But most importantly, I actually loved what I did!

So I reframed my thinking. I decided that work was actually a good thing. It not only provided me with money with which to buy the necessities of life, but it was fun. Fulfilling. A huge boost to my self-esteem.

I reframed my attitude about work. I decided I liked it. Instead of resisting it, I was going to throw myself into it. And I reframed my attitude about the company for which I worked. Instead of viewing it as a dark, sinister, stingy force that was impinging upon my life, I resolved to do everything in my power to help it succeed—to help make it the greatest advertising agency in the world.

I can't tell you what a difference those simple, basic attitude changes have made in my life in terms of income, self-esteem, confidence, and overall happiness. And I can't even begin to describe how much satisfaction I learned to take in the sheer act of work itself. As the saying goes, for me it's the most fun someone can have with their pants on. (Yes, I love golf every bit as much as I love work, but if I had to earn my living at it, I'd be homeless!)

You know, you often see this cute little aphorism on Internet jokes: "No one ever went to their deathbed wishing they'd spent more time at the office." I'm not so sure. Yes, family and friends and recreation bring us a great deal of pleasure. But don't underestimate the power of work to give you some of your greatest satisfactions.

So, my friend, switch the little attitude button that resides in your left frontal lobe. Turn it from Off—"I hate what I do and the company for which I do it"—and change it to On. And watch what an extraordinary change this can make in everything from your outlook on life to the kind of watch you're able to strap around your wrist.

Okay, now that we've taken the single most important step in becoming an indispensable employee, read on. We're now going to get into the tangible, practical, actionable, and, in many ways, very simple steps that will help you execute what it takes to quite quickly become indispensable.

Chapter Two

Ask Not What Your Company Can Do for You

This is the most important chapter in the entire book. In fact, if you can accept what's in this chapter—not just with your brain but with your heart, too—then you will have taken the first step on the ladder that leads up and out of the mass of ordinary employees—the ladder that leads to real success. So read this next sentence carefully: ASK NOT WHAT YOUR COMPANY CAN DO FOR YOU BUT RATHER WHAT YOU CAN DO FOR YOUR COMPANY. Read it again and again and again, because this, in a nutshell, is what becoming an indispensable employee is all about.

Every business leader I interviewed echoed this theme.

Whatever words they used, the meaning was unmistakably clear. Top executives are sick and tired of employees who can't seem to grasp that it is no longer business as usual. That today many companies are in a fight for their very existence. That things like raises, lengthy vacations, promotions, and bonuses may all have to be put on hold for quite some time. That hurt feelings, conflicts with other employees, grudges, personal distaste for certain assignments—all have to be temporarily swept aside in favor of your company's survival. This is not the time for the cult of the individual. This is the time for all of us to put our shoulders to the wheel for the greater good. Do you get it?

Over and over again, CEOs spoke of the importance of working with people who have the "right attitude," people who will come in and work on the weekend if necessary *(without* bitching), employees who'll stay and work an extra hour if it means meeting a deadline. Someone who's not the first out the door when the clock strikes five, someone who asks for more work when she's completed what's on her desk, someone who seems genuinely and sincerely interested in the well-being of the company. "We don't want someone whose primary concern is what the company can do for him or her," said one company president. "He should have enough confidence in himself not to worry about that. If his greatest concern is the fringe benefits, I wonder if he's just looking for a free ride. I like to see a person interested in what *she* can offer, how her long-range plans merge with the company's goals."

Here's how another chief executive looks at it: "Nothing irritates me more than the person who comes to work here with the idea that he's doing us a huge favor, that we're lucky to have him. During the dot-com boom, employees could get away with it. Business was good, and we took whoever we could get. Not anymore. In fact, we've never been so selective about the people we hire—and we're not doing very much hiring these days—and the people we keep. After all, the future of this company depends on people who are willing to give that little bit extra. The successful people have spent a good deal of time learning what they should be doing in their jobs, have gone beyond the basic job requirements, have a way of getting the cooperation of other workers; they're leaders. These are the people who will make the company grow and prosper—and we'll reward them for it. I get so damned enraged by employees who feel put upon when they have to extend themselves. We're all in this *together*—what benefits the company [in turn] benefits them. When they show their willingness to give that little bit extra, we realize that we need them!"

What's the moral of all this? It's simple. Show your boss and your company that you care. That you understand times are tough. That you're willing to roll up your sleeves and do whatever it takes to help your company survive and thrive. That you realize you may have to work longer and harder than ever before to help the company succeed—and that you're willing to do it *with a smile. The company's success—if you've had a part in it—can mean your success.* "As long as you're there anyway," said the chairman of the board of a large advertising agency, "why not really shoot for it? Why not be as good as you can be?" Why not?

I know that in your heart you may feel just the opposite. Don't worry about it. So do millions of other people—maybe even your boss. Keep these thoughts to yourself. Otherwise, you can expect a stagnant career, possibly even a layoff.

Think of it this way: You're leading a handful of people across the desert and there's barely enough drinking water to go around. Imagine how you would feel if someone started complaining about not being able to take his usual shower. Well, that's how bosses feel when they hear or even sense bitching and griping over a little extra work or a tighter budget. None of us can afford it these days.

Chapter Three

Think Long-term

Okay, here's an old-fashioned, upside-down, you've-got-to-be-kidding idea: Plan on staying with your present company for the rest of your career. Plan, in fact, on becoming CEO.

I know what you're thinking—*Who, me? That's ridiculous! I've got other plans. As soon as I put aside a few bucks, I'm going to quit and go to architecture school. Sign up for the Peace Corps. Write a screenplay. Move to Seattle and live a whole different kind of lifestyle.*

All right, fine. I hear where you're coming from. But right now, while you've got a job when hundreds of thousands are losing theirs, when you've got rent or a mortgage to take care of every month, when you're helping your aging mother pay for her meds, let's concentrate on doing the very best you can until the economy begins to heal and you're better able to fulfill your dreams. And one way to do that is to think ambitiously about rising to the very pinnacle of your company.

I fully understand we've become a culture that's radically changed its approach to company loyalty. Companies are no longer loyal to employees ... and employees are no longer loyal to companies. In the old days, people used to *assume* they would be working for the company they started with for their entire careers. You may even have a dad or an uncle who was with AT&T or Procter & Gamble for fifty years. No more. We take a new job today with the expectation that we'll only be there two or three years before moving on to something new and different. Not only do we change jobs every few years, we also expect to change career paths. You used to be in fashion. Now you're on to journalism. Started as a lawyer. Now you're a financial consultant. On one level it's a kind of natural evolution of the baby boomers' focus on "me"—the self. It's all about what *I* want to do.

Given all this, imagine how refreshing your boss will find it when you approach your job with a single-minded focus: *This is the place where I plan on spending the rest of my work life.* Even if you don't announce it as a fact, the people you report to will see it in your eyes, your attitude, your very approach to each and every assignment. You'll find yourself asking questions like: "But is this a product we can see ourselves selling fifteen years from now?" The positive feedback will be awesome. You'll quickly be seen as someone who has senior management potential, and you will be treated accordingly. Given more responsibility. Treated with increasing respect. Your ideas will be listened to with greater interest. And, of course, the more you're treated like this, the more positively you'll feel about your job. And the more positively you feel about your job, the more fun it'll be, the more you'll enjoy going into work. It's a cycle, and not a vicious one. In most cases you'll discover the more loyal you are to your employer, the more loyal she'll be to you.

Chapter Four

Make Your Company's Problems Your Own

An excellent way to become an indispensable employee is to develop an ability to solve your company's problems. To do this, of course, you have to know what they are.

How do you find out? You keep your ears open. What are the vice presidents talking about? Excessive labor costs? An inability to crack a certain market? Shoddy workmanship coming out of the factory? The rising cost of advertising? Sooner or later you're going to hear about the problems. They have a way of walking the halls.

Of course, you can also get a bird's-eye view of what's going on inside your company by simply searching for it on the Internet. Even a very small organization will probably have a whole raft of articles discussing it. Using the Internet to research the company for which you work is a good idea no matter what the economic climate. You'll be surprised how much you don't know about the place where you work—even if you've been there a dozen years. But during a recession, it's absolutely vital to know as much about your employer as possible. There are tons of articles out there on just about any company these days. You may discover that your employer is about to lay off the promotion department, is having trouble finding a good supplier of widgets, can't seem to get its website up. Knowing all this, of course, will give you a heads-up on where you can really have an impact.

But just in case you don't hear about the major problems, ask. That's right, *ask what they are*. Ask your direct supervisor, "Bob, what's keeping us from having a better year? How come profits are slumping? Why is our competition doing better than we are?" He'll tell you. Happily. One, because supervisors and bosses love to talk business; and two, because it will help relieve some of his anxiety. To share problems with others often seems to make them appear a little smaller. Your interest alone will make you appear more ambitious and will enhance your boss's estimation of you.

Okay, now that you know what your company's problems are, what can you do about them? You can help solve them, that's what. I know, you're probably thinking, *This guy's crazy*.

How can little old me solve this great big company's problems? I wouldn't know where to begin.

As with everything, there's nothing like beginning at the beginning. Set fifteen minutes aside every morning just to think about your company's problems. Read *Barron's*, *The Wall Street Journal*, a couple of trade publications. Surf the Net, bone up on your competition. What are the really successful companies in your field doing that your company isn't? Do some blue-sky thinking. Discuss it with your significant other (simply talking sometimes brings about inspiration and ideas). You may surprise yourself.

One company president told me how a nineteen-year-old secretary helped him solve one of his company's worst and most persistent problems. The company sold jewelry on college campuses by hiring local student representatives and paying them fifty dollars to distribute flyers on the campus. Those ordering the jewelry would do so by sending in the completed order blank and their check. The problem was that on many campuses the jewelry company was getting absolutely no orders, the reason being that the campus representative was pocketing the fifty dollars and then tossing the flyers into the nearest wastebasket. It was really stunting the profits of the company, because on the campuses where the flyers were being distributed, they rarely made a profit of less than sixty-eight hundred dollars.

Can you guess what the secretary's suggestion was? His idea was to pay the campus representatives no money up front, but instead give them a commission on each order the company received from the campus. How would the jewelry company know which campuses were generating which orders? Simply by keying the coupons—Ohio State would be OS, the University of Wisconsin would be UW, et cetera.

What were the results? An immediate 30 percent increase in sales and an almost total elimination of the problem of the flyers being thrown away. The campus representatives now realized that they had to work before getting paid.

What happened to the nineteen-year-old secretary? His boss made him his administrative assistant. That was eleven years ago. He is now the treasurer of the company and one of its largest stockholders—all because he made his company's problems his own.

Chapter Five

Be a "Can-Do" Person

More than a few chief executives mentioned how irked they get when they're given a million reasons why something *can't* be done—there's not enough time, it's physically impossible, we'd have to do it over again, it's never been done that way before. "There's only one way you can and should act with a difficult assignment," said one. "With a very positive attitude. Even though the prospects may look dark and dreary, you can't let that show. You must be very upbeat, put on your thinking cap, and start coming up with ideas, questions to be asked, answers. Find out where you're going and what you're doing, and do it with verve and élan, even if your insides are tearing out. You must always wear a positive attitude and never admit defeat."

You have to remember, a person who gets to be the head of a company is probably pretty smart. When he asks you to do something that is difficult, he's not daydreaming or asking for the moon. He's probably asking for something that actually can be done, even if at first it sounds impossible to you. It's something that, if he were asked to do it, he would find a way to get it done. So don't automatically reject his request. Don't rack your brain for a million different reasons why it can't be done. Instead, tell him you'll get right to work on it. You're not 100 percent sure it can be done, but if there's a way to do it, you'll find it.

Believe me, particularly when the going gets tough, bosses like to have "can-do" people around them.

Chapter Six

Be a Great Team Player

You can be the world's most efficient worker, put in fourteen hours a day, and know everything there is to know about your company and the industry—but if you can't get along with your colleagues, you're not going to be worth much to your company.

Every executive I interviewed mentioned getting along with other workers as one of the fundamental strengths of an indispensable employee. As trite as this may sound, a company is a team—and a team can't be very effective if its members are expending their energy on clashing with each other rather than on contributing to the team effort.

For one thing, in business there's simply no *time* for personal problems between employees. The company is there to produce a product or a service and make a profit, and time that the boss has to spend arbitrating arguments between his subordinates is time taken away from attending to company business.

The boss doesn't know about your disagreement with the guy at the next desk, you say? Of course he knows! He gets feedback all the time from people you come in contact with during the course of a day. "If people bitch and complain, if they put on airs, are arrogant, [or] fail to understand fellow workers' problems, it comes back to me," said one top executive. "By observing and listening, you get a pretty good picture of who can get along with other people and who can't. An employee who's out of step with his colleagues soon finds out it's not appreciated—and either he changes his attitude or he changes jobs."

Getting along with people also makes you a better worker, because you're open to input from your colleagues, input that you wouldn't get if you were standoffish or belligerent.

Obviously, you can motivate others when you relate well to them, when you're friendly and cooperative. And that will be noticed. "Your fellow employees will bring you to my attention by looking up to you, coming to you with questions, speaking well of you," says the head of a law firm. "And if you can bring opposing factions together and get them to sit and talk and cooperate rather than be at each other's throats, you're a very valuable person."

Finally, your superiors will feel comfortable making you the head of a team, because they'll know you won't let your own temperament get in the way of doing the job. "You can have terrific ability to do the job," said the general manager of a sizable real estate concern, "but if you can't cooperate with other workers, what's it worth? I'll take the person with the terrific personality over the one with high ability and a lousy personality. We only fired one person in the past several years, and that was because she simply didn't know how to get along with other workers."

Of course, you don't have to be everybody's best friend all the time. In fact, if you spend *too* much of your energy chatting with other employees, you may get a reputation as a gossip or a busybody. You certainly don't want to spread tales about one employee to others; be discreet, and be wary of giving out personal information about yourself or others, because you don't know how discreet other people will be.

And unless someone has done something clearly dishonest or harmful to the company, never complain to the boss about a fellow employee; rather than appreciating your zeal for monitoring other people's performance, she'll take it as a sign that you can't get along with others, that you're not a good team player.

If you thought yours was a lonely climb to the top, think again. Your fellow employees are very much a part of the picture, and you need every one of them. You don't have to be isolated and standoffish to succeed. You *can* be friendly and allow yourself to like your coworkers. In fact, it will even benefit you in your quest to become indispensable.

Some Critical "Don'ts"

Chapter Seven

Winning Without Intimidation

You may think that the indispensable employee, the man or woman who succeeds in today's fiercely competitive job market, has to be the aggressive, ruthless type who doesn't care how many people he steps on to get to the top. Maybe you've read some of the classic pop psych books on looking out for number one, power and how to get it, winning through intimidation, and so on. But what if that's just not you? Suppose you like people and aren't willing to climb to success over the wreckage of other people's jobs. Is it possible for a decent human being, who believes in treating others fairly, to get ahead?

Absolutely! You can win without intimidation, without

disregard for other people or their reactions to you. And you can begin to do it now.

Not one of the top executives I interviewed even mentioned intimidation or ruthlessness as qualities they wanted in their employees. In fact, all the qualities they mentioned were basically positive ones: they want decent, honest, dedicated, hard-working people who can get along with others. So don't worry if you're not as abrasive and domineering as the person you're competing with for the next promotion.

This person will do everything he can to make you believe he's way ahead of you in the race; that's his style. By keeping your good-natured, thoughtful approach, you'll swiftly (and more comfortably!) move well past him.

Chapter Eight

Don't Lead (or Join) a Company Revolt

You won't make any friends among your superiors if all you do is complain. Employees are always complaining—pay's too low, vacations are too short, benefits are lousy, work's too hard—and because discontent tends to be contagious, it's very easy to let yourself get stoked up about these things.

Rule number uno: *When you feel yourself getting involved in negativism, walk away.* Don't sign petitions or join a strike, even though there may at first seem to be strength in numbers and the cause may seem justified. During harsh economic times, joining any kind of revolt against the hand that feeds you is doomed to fail, and it will almost certainly taint your reputation in the eyes of your employer.

If you fail to get the raise you want, if working conditions are less than perfect, if you're asked to do something above and beyond the call of duty—complain about it and you may soon find yourself out of a job, or at least out of the running for further responsibility and promotions when the economy improves.

On the other hand, if you can show your boss or supervisor that you're a mature person, someone capable of accepting a difficult or distressing development without going to pieces, he will think more highly of you.

The president of a medium-sized children's clothing company told me that recently he had to deny his sales force an expected raise in their commissions. He called them together in one big meeting at a hotel, and then he let them have the bad news as gently as possible. He told them it was a question of the future of the company. Costs were rising so high that at this time it was simply impossible to give them the promised raise.

"The reaction," he told me, "was a nightmare. Half the people wanted to walk out right then and there. Others started yelling at me. I tell you, I came close to firing the whole damn lot of them right on the spot. Here I am, trying to keep the company in good shape, and all they do is insult me.

"All except one guy. A salesman in our New England territory. He stands up and says, 'Hey, what the hell's the matter with you guys? Don't you know Mr. Schaefer is doing this because he has to? We're making good money. We can afford a little delay. Let's stop bitching and just get out there and sell. Hell, with a little bit of luck our sales will be up enough to make up for the raise we haven't got yet.'

"I tell you, I could have kissed that man. I don't want people in my company who are going to hate me, or hate the company, or go completely sour on us just because times are tough. I want hard-hitting, mature people who can carry on in the face of adversity. I want realistic people who can understand basic recession-time business logic.

"And wouldn't you know it, that salesman from New England is one of our best, most aggressive salesmen. It always seems to work that way. The people who really do a great job are almost always the really great people."

Be a great person yourself. Even if the company does some things that bring you down, *don't lose your determination to do an outstanding job*. Your company will definitely notice, and will appreciate you for it.

Chapter Nine

Don't Run Scared

During tough times like these, many employees walk around wearing their fear on their sleeves. They're transparent. One sideways look from the boss, and they immediately fall into a panic. The next second they're hovering around the boss's office, looking for a good sign, a kind word, something, anything, to reassure them that they're not in jeopardy.

This kind of behavior is not recommended for those who want to be indispensable. First of all, panic is contagious. If your behavior reveals that you lack confidence in your job security, your boss will pick up on it. Fast. And it won't be very reassuring to her. She'll think: If this guy's so nervous about keeping his job, he must have a guilty conscience. Maybe he's goofing off, or screwing up. Maybe he thinks he's lousy at what he does. I'd better take a closer look at him.

"Running scared" also saps both your energy and your time. If you're walking around all day in an absolute panic about whether you're going to last the week, you'll waste a lot of energy that could be used in doing great work.

Don't give in to panic. Work at appearing confident about your job even if at first you feel as if you're just acting. Make a conscious effort to walk tall, hold your head high, look people directly in the eye, speak in a firm voice. Don't worry out loud about your position or the company's future. If you're under a lot of stress, find ways to reduce it outside the office—regular exercise like jogging or swimming is terrific, as are meditation, yoga, and other relaxation techniques. Do nice things for yourself whenever you can—a relaxing movie, a dinner out, a weekend trip. Talk about your fears to your significant other or close friends, *not* to coworkers or your boss. Most of all, think positively. You're going to keep your job, for as long as you want it, because you do it better than any other person in the world.

I know it may be tough in an economy like this, but *now more than ever is the time to project an aura of competence and firm belief in yourself.* Don't forget, a bad economy also makes your boss nervous. He'll find it soothing and comforting to have employees around him who make him feel that everything's going to turn out all right.

Chapter Ten

Be Smart—Not Too Smart

Are you smarter than your boss?

Then terrific! Put your brain to work and do a great job at whatever you're doing. But don't, under any circumstance, try to prove to your boss that you're twice as smart as he is. He won't like it.

Why do I bring this subject up in the first place? Because some very bright people feel compelled (for reasons I'll never fully understand) to prove that they are smarter than their boss *to* their boss. I suppose they get some sort of ego satisfaction out of this. But you can be sure their boss doesn't.

The head of an advertising agency told me that once or twice a year she'll wind up hiring a young MBA whiz kid who expends most of his energy proving that he's smarter than the management supervisor to whom he's been assigned. As soon as the agency head gets wind of this, she calls the young MBA into her office and reams him. Her concern is that anybody who has an instinct to show up his boss will almost certainly have an instinct to show up his client. And in advertising, there's no faster way to lose a piece of business than to show up your client. "I try to make him understand," says the agency head, "that he should concentrate on using his genius on the job at hand rather than to develop new and exciting ways to show everyone how brilliant he is. If he doesn't get the message," she went on, "I fire him. I don't care how smart someone is. If they can't use their brains to get along well with others as they do their job, then to me they're just plain stupid."

When times are good and companies are desperate to fill slots, maybe you can get away with being a wiseass. But when times are tough, some bosses are just looking for reasons to fire an employee they don't particularly like. Want to be really smart? Make your *boss* feel smart. You can be sure of one thing—*an employee who makes his boss feel smart will go a lot further than one who makes his boss feel stupid.*

Chapter Eleven

Know How to Fight for Your Ideas

There's been a great deal written in various business publications about the employee who stands up uncompromisingly proud, fierce, and committed to her ideas, and in the end triumphs. Well, that makes great copy. But in real life it rarely happens that way. First of all, the employee who stands up for her ideas might be wrong. And even if she isn't, that's still no guarantee that she'll impress her boss. The fact is that most bosses don't want to be disagreed with beyond a certain point.

The CEO of an Atlanta radio station told me that after a while he just tunes out when an employee keeps arguing with him. "I've been at this for close to ten years," he said. "I've come to know what kind of music our audience likes. Yet some of my younger DJs are always trying to get me to play 'alternative' music. They tell me I'm a dork, that the audience is evolving. I listen for a while, explain my point, and when they keep pressing the issue, I finally say, 'Get the hell out of my office.' In truth, I find it insulting when someone who's been in the business less than a year thinks he knows more about our audience than I do."

He doesn't mind when people who work for him suggest other ways of doing things if they feel they've found a better way. He listens to their suggestions carefully, he says. But if, after weighing the pros and cons of each idea, he still decides to have things done his way, he doesn't want any further discussion of the matter. Those employees who persist in pressing their point, instead of accepting his, are making a big mistake. If they keep it up, he gives them a blunt warning. If they still harp on it, he lets them go.

"I'm not a dictator," he says. "Far from it. I've gotten some terrific ideas from my employees, ideas that at first seemed crazy or without much potential. But people who try to put themselves on the map by being overly aggressive and argumentative quickly turn me off. They're simply not worth the trouble, no matter how competent they are."

All the executives I interviewed mentioned their willingness to listen to their employees' opinions. "I feel that the people who are out there doing their job know more about their work than I do," said one. "What I'm mainly concerned about is this: Is their disagreement with me based on what they think will be good for the company? If so, I respect that. I may throw cold water on it or reject it, but I welcome it. But if I think they're disagreeing simply because it's good for *them*, I have a very different attitude about it, and I tell them so in no uncertain terms."

Arguing for the sake of arguing is no good. And any arguing should always be done in the privacy of an office, not in front of other people.

The point of this chapter is not to scare you, or to get you to keep your mouth shut even though you're convinced that your company's making a foolish move. The moral here is that after a point, your arguing will do more damage than good. Bosses tend to be pretty savvy people. When they want something done in a certain way, they probably have a good reason for it . . . even if at first that reason isn't apparent to you. If you disagree, let your boss know about it, strongly and firmly. If she still isn't open to it, then let it drop. Do it her way. Don't make a pain in the neck of yourself. It can only get you in trouble.

Chapter Twelve

Don't Be an "Injustice Collector"

An alternate title for this chapter could have been "How to Get Over the Raise/Bonus/Promotion You Didn't Get and Get On with Your Job."

I mean it, buddy. Get over it. Now. *For good.*

I don't know what it is about the human psyche, but in a perverse way we sometimes seem to enjoy a setback better than a victory.

Remember when you were a kid and your parents sent you up to your room—unjustly, you thought—for something your little brother did? You wept buckets of tears, and when your folks finally said you could come down, you didn't really want to. You'd been having too good of a time wallowing in self-pity.

That may have been okay when you were a kid, but it's unproductive, self-indulgent, self-destructive, and even dangerous at work.

At work, you are a marine, not a collector of injustices. You take a hit, get over it, and keep moving forward.

I can't tell you how many employees have poured out their hearts to me about promotions they didn't get three and even five years ago. They're obsessed with these injustices, remembering them with excruciating detail. I ask myself, how can they have any energy for their jobs when they're so mired in the past?

Now I don't mean to ask the inhuman of you. I'm not suggesting you absorb a blow with no reaction whatsoever. In fact, it's *important* to react. But do it this way: seek out your partner, spouse, boyfriend, girlfriend, therapist, a close relative—*not* someone at work. Vent fully and completely, with all the rage and hurt you feel. Then put it behind you, even if it still smarts, and throw yourself back into your job. That's an order.

There's no faster way to get the next raise/bonus/promotion you think you deserve than simply to forget about the one you didn't get.

Chapter Thirteen

Don't Abuse Your Expense Account

During the rich, ripe latter part of the nineties, I knew of a company that actually encouraged people to go hog wild with their expense accounts. If you asked for a raise, and you weren't quite due for one, they'd stave you off by telling you to take it out on your expense account. "Put in for a few extra cab rides and a late dinner or two every week," they'd tell you. "At least until you're officially due that raise."

You know something? They're not doing that anymore. In fact, today they go over expense accounts with a fine-toothed comb. And if they find anything that looks even the slightest bit fishy, they disallow it. Automatically. There's simply no appealing the ruling.

Furthermore, the company as a whole frowns upon employees who run up big expense accounts, even if the employee can seemingly justify it. Said the executive vice president of a successful real estate company: "Our company definitely looks on keeping expense accounts down as a plus factor—we consciously watch it and make sure it doesn't become a drain on the cash flow. With government regulations getting stiffer, you have to account for everything."

What's the moral of this story? With money as tight as it is, I believe you're hurting yourself more than it's worth if you're fudging a few extra bucks on your expense account. Today, even presidents of companies are reviewing expense accounts. And they don't take kindly to those that seem out of line. "You'd better have a damn good explanation for everything," said one, "or it'll come out of your hide." In fact, they may even look upon it as stealing. So take my advice: Don't do it. It just isn't worth it.

Chapter Fourteen

Don't Waste Company Supplies

There are two reasons for this. The first is that wasting anything is unecological and unethical. The second is that, in many ways, wasting company paper clips and copy paper and file folders and pens and cartons and whatever other supplies your company uses is equal to wasting company money. In tough times like these, nothing could be worse. Even small wastage can add up.

If your boss or supervisor sees you being wantonly wasteful, you can be sure he won't like it. It'll give the boss a bad feeling about you and can negate some excellent achievements on your part.

The chief executive of an advertising agency reported that

she lost all interest in a brilliant young account executive when she saw him throw away half a dozen partially used yellow legal pads. It was right at the end of a successful meeting with an important client at which the young account executive had distinguished himself. The young man was helping to tidy up the meeting room and absentmindedly chucked the pads into the wastebasket. He didn't realize at the time that he was also tossing away his career at that agency.

The head of a law firm told me that she personally instructed all of her employees not to waste paper, and she was particularly impressed and gratified when a young paralegal came to her with the idea of using the blank back pages of old memos as new memos.

So don't waste anything—not even rubber bands. And if you can think of a way to save your company extra money by making better use of supplies, let your boss know about it. It's the kind of thinking that will really make a good impression.

Time
Management

Chapter Fifteen

Take It One Assignment at a Time

A recent article in the business section of a prestigious newspaper said Americans are getting in earlier, leaving the office later, putting in more hours, and getting less done.

I wasn't sure I agreed, until I looked around me and watched how the people I work with handle their assignments. It seems that we've never been busier, yet I'm not all that sure that our output is really any greater.

I've had group managers come to my office in a panic, near tears, overwhelmed with their workload. I always say, "Calm down. Tell me the single most important assignment you have. Now what do you need to do to complete it?" This decided, we go on to the second most important assignment. And so on. It's astonishing what a soothing effect this always has, and how much less daunting the workload seems.

One of the most useful pieces of advice I've ever gotten was this: *Handle each chore only once.* This means once you have picked up a piece of paper from your desk, do everything that must be done so you'll never have to look at it again. Take the task as far as you can take it. The reason we're so busy but getting less done is that we're always picking up papers, agonizing over them, and putting them back down on the other side of the desk, only to have to pick them up and agonize again later. At the end of a day like that, it's often hard to say that you've really accomplished anything.

If you have a particularly heinous task to accomplish, do it when you're freshest, and promise yourself that you won't stop doing it until you never have to think about it again. You'll surprise yourself when you see that it wasn't as bad as you thought it would be, and you'll feel rewarded with a great sense of accomplishment.

I've found that in life there is almost always time for everything if you don't panic, if you take on one chore at a time and apply a quality hour against it, giving it your undivided attention, without peering anxiously over your shoulder at other assignments.

Of course, while I may have become skilled at helping

others, I sometimes do get overwhelmed myself. I've found that it helps to voice my concerns aloud to my assistant. He always says, "What's the single most important thing to get done first?"

In stressful times like these, it's important to keep from running around like a headless chicken. One of the best ways to do that is to seek the ear of a colleague, spouse, partner, or supervisor who can help you prioritize your assignments. We're often much better at helping defuse someone else's anxiety than we are at dealing with our own. But the fact is, if we take it one solid step at a time, there is almost nothing we can't accomplish.

Chapter Sixteen

Ask for More Work

Here's something that you may very well hate to do, but I can't exaggerate how important it can be in your efforts to become an indispensable employee. So if you're a good worker and can get work done quickly, I recommend that once you've completed your assignments, rather than sit there sending texts to your friends while waiting to receive your next project, you ask for more work.

Even in a stringent economy like this, there is often a lot of downtime, time when employees are sitting around on their hands. Company presidents hate this. "I can't distribute work so evenly and so skillfully that all my attorneys are busy all the time," the chief partner of a law firm told me. "Some have too much work at times and others have nothing to do for as long as a week at a time. And you know something? I resent it when someone has nothing to do and doesn't come in and tell me about it. I feel they're cheating me. I don't pay them to sit around on their duffs. I always have a million assignments in the wings, but sometimes I just don't have the time to assign them to people, or in the rush I forget about them—they're not at the top of my mind because I have more immediate things to get done. And yet these projects are damned important.

"So, if someone comes in and says, 'Boss, I just finished my brief on the Rosendahl case. What else do you have for me to do?' I'll give her one of these future projects and I'll also be damned impressed. I'll say to myself, There's a woman who wants to get ahead, who cares about this firm, who's not just out to get as much as she can for as little work as possible. I like to have people around me who want to work as hard as I do."

It's that *thirst* for work that impresses just about every chief executive I spoke to. At work, there are two things you must never say: "I'm too busy" and "That isn't my job"—even if you are in fact justified in saying them. Your boss will hate it—and will remember it when you're up for a raise or promotion, or worse, when there's a need to trim staff. These statements suggest that you feel burdened, that you think the boss is asking too much of you. "If we ask someone to take on extra work," said a high-ranking officer of a gigantic packaged goods company, "we don't want to hear, 'This isn't in my job description.' We feel that we do right by our employees, we care about each one of them, and in return we expect them to help out when we need them. When *they* are really overburdened with work, we will ask someone else to lighten *their* load a bit." There is one exception here. If you're certain that your boss is totally unaware of the enormity of your workload, and you don't think she would give you another assignment if she were, let her know what you're currently working on. If she still asks you to take on more work, do so willingly.

The really successful people in business don't wait to be *asked* to do extra work. They are constantly volunteering to take on more responsibility—especially when the extra work helps them develop their skills or gives them an opportunity to show what they can do. But even when it is just routine, run-of-the-mill work, they make sure their superiors know they are willing—more than that, *eager*—to take it on.

There is only one caution I should mention in connection with this point. It's possible, although not probable, that your boss could think: If this guy doesn't have enough work, maybe I should fire him. Maybe we have too many people around here. Therefore, if you do drop in on the boss to ask for more work, let him know how busy you've been and how busy you will be in two days hence. A smart boss will check into your work to see if it's being done properly and on time, and if you do in fact need more work. That way he'll realize that things are only temporarily slow for you, and that most of the time you've got your hands full. He'll then be impressed that even though you had the chance to take a short and obviously deserved breather, you chose to give your all to the company and asked for more work.

"If you do more than you're being compensated to do," said the publisher of a top magazine, "it gets noticed."

Chapter Seventeen

Meet Deadlines

Here's a subject the company leaders I interviewed couldn't stress enough: GET YOUR WORK DONE ON TIME! They said that employees who meet deadlines, come rain or come shine, are worth their weight in gold.

One company president told me that the very survival of her company depends on its ability to promise to do a job quickly and then make good on that promise. It is what gives her company an advantage over the competition. She feels the key to getting work done quickly is the willingness of the people who work for her to do whatever has to be done to get the job completed on time, no matter what the obstacles, no matter how hard they have to work.

"Right now I've got a foreman," she said, "who is literally as important to the company as I am. When he homes in on a job, that's all that exists for him. Nothing gets in his way. I know when I give him a rush assignment that it'll get done on time. He may have to push the people under him. He may have to work straight through the night himself. But the job will get done."

Here's a great way to become an indispensable employee. If your business is like most, your boss depends on meeting certain deadlines. Show her that you can bring the toughest assignment in on time. *Every time!* She won't be able to get along without you.

How do you accomplish something like that? You commit yourself to it. Passionately. You tell your assistant he's going to have to work overtime to help you. You come in early. You stay late. You tell your partner or spouse that you're going to be concentrating on a very important assignment for the next couple of days and you need support and understanding. You may be late for dinner, you may be irritable around the house, but you've got to get it done.

What else can you do to make sure you meet the deadline? Make a checklist of things you must do to complete the project and then make sure you're doing them as quickly and efficiently as possible. Try not to get sidetracked. If you can avoid it, don't take on any additional assignments during this time. Concentrate all your energies and talents on getting the job done on time. Make it a personal crusade.

One of the most effective ways to make sure you meet all your deadlines is to make it a firm policy to complete all assignments ahead of time. That's right, at *least* a couple days ahead of time. The company presidents I spoke to all told me how much they love getting work back earlier than expected. It not only makes them feel that you're competent, devoted, and eager for responsibility, but it actually fills them with a personal sense of achievement—all of which will make you indispensable.

Remember when you ran relay races in school? The team captains tried to get the fastest runners on their team, and to keep the slow members off. The same thing goes on in business. Obviously, the slow members of the corporate team slow the whole group down, and the super-fast ones increase the team's chances of being number one.

So next time you get an assignment, try completing it ahead of time. This way, if you should run into a snag, at least you'll meet your deadline. You'll also be making yourself a truly indispensable employee.

Chapter Eighteen

Take Work Home with You

Here's a way to keep up with the extra workload many of us are facing now that companies are trying to get more out of each and every employee. Take work home with you. I know the idea may initially sound depressing and almost too much to bear. After all, you work hard all day long. You work harder and more intensely than ever before. So the last thing you need is for me to tell you to take work home.

And yet I feel compelled to mention it. One, because it can help you keep up with a workload that is so heavy you can't do it justice even working a longer day. Two, because it can help you get ahead and become more indispensable to your company. And three, because so many of us waste time at home at night watching dopey television shows or just aimlessly surfing the Internet, playing solitaire or online poker, or looking at porn—a huge waste of time.

My feeling is this: If you're going to sit in front of the television set, glued to a show that taxes only 3 percent of your entire brain, why not keep a trade publication on your lap? Or the *Wall Street Journal?* When the show gets too slow, or a commercial comes on, read a couple of paragraphs. Who knows, you could come up with a great idea right then and there.

"I'm baffled by people who *don't* take work home," said one executive I interviewed. "In our industry it's impossible to get through all the reading during business hours. It's a given to do a couple of hours' reading on the weekend." One company president told me he made it a ritual to read business publications for forty-five minutes every single weekday night. He found them stimulating and interesting and often the source of some very innovative and profitable ideas. Why can't you do the same thing? It's not boring, and may not even seem like work. And it may turn you into a real genius at the office.

You want to become an indispensable employee? A half hour of homework every night will have you well on your way.

Chapter Nineteen

Get In on Time
(or Even Early)

This sounds so ridiculously basic that I hesitate to mention it; yet all the company presidents I interviewed put it near the top of their lists. *They want their employees in on time.* And that doesn't mean fifteen to twenty minutes late.

If your office officially opens at nine o'clock, get in at nine. Or ten minutes early. Or even an hour early! As times get tougher it's going to be the employee who does more than he's asked who keeps his job. And getting in early is one simple way to show your boss you're ready to do more. I find I'm much sharper in the morning. I usually get in around seven thirty, an hour and a half to two hours before the storm hits. This lets me program my day ahead of time. It lets me direct events rather than have them direct me.

One top-ranking executive I spoke with said she wanders up and down the halls two or three mornings a week at eight thirty (the office doesn't officially open until nine) to see who's in. She's impressed by those people she finds at their desks. "They don't have to be in early," she told me, "and that's precisely what impresses me. When someone thinks enough of his or her job, cares enough about the company to get a jump on the day, to get some important work done before the phones begin ringing, I think to myself, 'There's someone who has the character and the drive we need during tough times.' I don't want a lot of playboys or part-time workers. I want people who take their jobs seriously. And when I see a person sitting at her desk at eight thirty in the morning answering her e-mails or dictating memos, I know she takes her job seriously." Getting in early may be the most cliched characteristic of the dedicated employee, but it still works—and don't forget it.

You say you have trouble getting in on time. I've got a simple little trick for you. Set your alarm clock forty-five minutes earlier than you usually do. Then, even if you dawdle, or get caught in traffic, or take an extra-long shower, you'll still be in on time.

"The tradition at our company is to get in on time or earlier," said one executive vice president. "If someone didn't, that alone might not be reason for dismissal, but if there were other weaknesses in his performance, consistent lateness—of even a few minutes—might be the deciding factor."

Sure, I know it's tough giving up that extra delicious sleep. But think of all the nights you'll be up worrying if you find yourself out of a job. And besides, once you get used to getting in early, you'll be surprised how easy it is and how much more pleasant it makes your job. When you get a good start on the day's work, it helps you feel less rushed and harried. I wouldn't do it any other way.

Chapter Twenty

Eat Lunch at Your Desk

I can't think of one single reason to recommend eating a big lunch unless you want to waste the entire afternoon. Big lunches are time consuming, cost a lot of money, make you fat, groggy, and, if you have too much to drink, possibly even drunk. None of these things is constructive to the man or woman who wants to become an indispensable employee.

For the past ten years I've eaten about 90 percent of my lunches at my desk. I found a good sandwich shop with an excellent variety of food and almost always order from there. I eat slowly and leisurely, and yet lunch rarely takes me half an hour. Then, if I feel the need for new sights and inspirations, I take a walk. I find a brisk twenty-minute walk can work wonders to free one's mind and body; unlike a big, heavy lunch, it makes you trimmer, healthier, and more energetic.

In some kinds of work, quick, on-the-job lunches are not only desirable, they're essential. "Most of my employees take five-minute lunches," says one CEO. "We have a six-hour trading day on the stock exchange and can't afford long lunches. News items impact us immediately, and our people have to be here. If you're out to lunch when an important piece of news comes in, you really don't belong in this business."

I fully understand that some of you are accustomed to at least an hour break during the middle of the day. And still others may feel a crushing sense of gloom at the thought of not being able to indulge in a lengthy, full-course meal. *What else is there in life*, I can hear them saying.

Well, all I can answer is that these are times in which many speak of "belt tightening" and "cutting the fat." These are more than just catchphrases. Companies are belt tightening and fat cutting by terminating hundreds and thousands of people. If you don't want to be one of them, you're just going to have to suck it up and make some radical changes. This is what maturing is all about—learning how to do what needs to be done, even if you don't like it one bit.

Think of it this way. Want to stay employed? Want to get ahead? Want to make the most of your day? Want to have a bright, productive afternoon? Then skip the big, heavy lunch and have a sandwich at your desk. You'll save calories, money, and maybe even your job.

Chapter Twenty-one

Stay Until the Job is Done

The president of a small chain of drugstores told me that one of the things that annoys her most about certain employees is that they often go home right in the middle of a rush assignment. "Sometimes I can't believe my eyes," she went on. "I ask one of my young executives to draw up a certain report for me on this or that. I let him know I need it right away. What happens? The clock strikes five and I don't have the report. I look in the guy's office, and there's no sign of him. I look at his computer screen, and I see that he's left off right in the *middle* of the document. Obviously, he plans to finish it in the morning. Well, that just doesn't sit well with me. I like a guy or gal who digs right in and doesn't go home until they've finished the report. I stay until six thirty or seven o'clock at night, and I damn well expect the people who want to get ahead in my company to do the same thing—especially if I let them know I need something right away.

"Now I realize, of course, that sometimes people have doctor's appointments or dinner engagements. And that's fine. But if they do, then they should check in with me before they go home and let me know where they are on the assignment, why they can't finish it that night, and what time they plan to have it on my desk the next morning."

"We have a saying here," said the chairman of the board of a major newspaper. "The hours *is* until the work *isn't*." Another executive expanded on the theme: "A really good employee doesn't even ask if she should come early or stay late—she's there! She *knows* she has to stay until the job is completed. You don't have to poke and prod and say, 'Hey, Cheryl, you promised me this two weeks ago.' Of course, we know there are only so many hours in the day, and we don't push anybody beyond their capacity to perform. And I respect someone who's smart enough to say, 'Listen, I gave it all I had and I'm wiped out.' That means she has the brains to know her performance will suffer if she goes on, damaging her health or the job. You can sense when someone's giving their all. I had a very excellent foreman once—the equipment wasn't the best, and he was the only one who knew how to keep the presses going, even if it had to be with rubber bands and chewing gum. To make sure we were going in the right direction, he'd come in at six a.m. and stay till midnight if necessary. No one asked him to do that; he just did it on his own."

The moral of this story is very simple: If you get a rush assignment, complete it before you go home, even if it means delaying or canceling evening plans. Nothing impresses a boss more than an employee who sticks with a chore until it's done. Executive after executive stressed this point. "One of the worst things," said one, "is someone who's always checking the time, and at three minutes to five is already straightening up their desk. Our estimate of that person goes down several notches in terms of increases, advancement, merit raises, et cetera. But if there's an emergency, a computer breakdown or something, and I say to someone, 'Will you stay till seven or eight tonight?'—if there's an immediate, willing 'Yes,' those are the people we want to keep."

"I look for people prepared to go beyond nine to five in doing a job right," said a magazine publisher. "Promotions in our company are based not only on how well someone has performed, but on how committed and dedicated they are. Do they have the desire to do the job right, no matter how much time it takes?"

Finally, let me share with you a story one company president told me: "I'll give you a tip my first secretary gave me, twenty-five years ago," he said. "I used to leave the office about five fifteen, five thirty, and she'd always still be working. I said, 'Jane, what are you doing?' We'd gotten to know each other on a fairly informal basis by then, and she said, 'At business school they told me, "Always leave five minutes after the boss; it'll impress him."' And you know what? It worked!" Try it. You'll be surprised and delighted at how pleased your boss will be.

Chapter Twenty-two

Delay Your Vacation
if Necessary

This is going to be a most unpopular suggestion, especially with partners, spouses, and children, yet three of the ten company presidents I interviewed said they felt it was important. If you've got a vacation planned and a crucial piece of work comes up that could best be handled by you, now is the time to delay that vacation. I know it's tough. I know it's heartbreaking. I know it's murder if there are family members or friends whom you've made plans with. But still, it's just one more of those things that can help make you an indispensable employee.

One chief executive told me that the day before one of his employees was about to leave for a two-week vacation to

Bermuda, the company acquired a new piece of business—the kind of business in which that employee specialized. You know what happened? The employee immediately marched into his boss's office and said he was quite willing to delay his vacation because he realized how profitable that new piece of business was going to be to the company. As it turned out, the new account took a couple of weeks to become formally settled, so the man was able to go to Bermuda as scheduled. But you can imagine the impression his willingness to delay his vacation made on his boss: "I tell you, when Rob came zooming in like that, I was bowled over. I'm not sure I would have even asked him to do it, but the very fact that he volunteered warmed my heart. That's the kind of person I want working for my company."

Also, if you do have a vacation coming up and there doesn't seem to be a conflict with work, don't sneak out on the day you leave. Let all your supervisors and bosses know you're going on vacation. During times like these it won't be appreciated if you zip out of the office for two or three weeks without letting people know when and where you're going. I realize, of course, that you increase your chances of getting someone else's overload of work, or of being called back from your vacation. But, after all, this isn't a book about enjoying yourself. It's a book about hanging on to and excelling at your job, no matter how bad the times get.

And one of the ways to do that is to be flexible about your vacation plans.

One last thought. Instead of insisting on an extended vacation because you're owed a couple of weeks, why not take more, shorter vacations, three- and four-day weekends? Many find this approach more genuinely restorative, and it's less of a strain on your company, particularly if you're in a position of importance. I have an employee whose job it is to enter our films into all the important festivals. Recently, he took his entire allotment of vacation—a month—all at once. While he was away, we missed the deadline of several truly significant festivals, ones that acquisitions people from all the movie studios attend. It made me realize that I simply cannot have the key players in my company out of the office for extended periods of time. I have since set up a policy to prevent it from happening again.

Chapter Twenty-three

Be On Call 24/7

This is really easy. I'm almost certain you've got a laptop, a cell phone, an iPhone, a BlackBerry—probably more than one of the above, or maybe even all of them. Whatever the combination, simply have a business card printed up with ALL your contact information on it and hand it out to your boss, your supervisors, human resources, your important colleagues, your assistant or secretary, if you have one. And when you do, let each and every one of them know that you are wholeheartedly, enthusiastically, on call 24/7.

When you go on a vacation or are leaving on a business trip, once again remind your boss and supervisors that you are on call, no matter where you are, 24 hours a day, 7 days a week. It's just one more way to let them know that you take your job more seriously than any other employee in the company.

Making Yourself "Recession-Proof"

Chapter Twenty-four

Get to Know Your Boss

Do you know your boss? I don't mean just his name, or where he sits, or what he looks like. I mean, do you know him personally? Do you feel free to walk into his office and chat with him? If you meet him on the street, do you know him well enough to fall into step beside him and talk with him all the way to the office?

What happens if you meet your boss at the corner luncheonette? Do you have a close enough relationship to sit down at her table and talk about what's going on back at the office? Some companies have policies that encourage this kind of personal give-and-take, such as monthly coffee-and-bagel meetings between the boss and a randomly selected group of employees. But if your company doesn't, and if your answers to the above questions are negative, or you're not sure, I have a suggestion: Get to know your boss better than you do now. It's important, not just to your career in general, but because in times like these it'll be a lot harder for your boss to fire someone he knows personally and feels reasonably close to than to fire a half-recognizable face from down the hall.

"I want my employees to seek me out," said one executive. "My door's always open."

Many people worry about getting on the boss's nerves, or that they'll appear like sycophants if they make a concerted effort to get close to the boss. Well, I won't deny that these are real dangers, but I am convinced that it's even more dangerous to be an almost total stranger to the man or woman who's leading your department or company. An ad agency executive advises: "You want to know what makes that person tick: Why is she in that job? Personal contact is tremendously important in business." After all, if you do something brilliant, you sure as hell want your boss to realize it was you who did it. If she only vaguely knows who you are, it's that much more difficult for your triumph to penetrate her consciousness. She'll recognize your name a whole lot faster and more vividly if she's heard it before and knows you personally.

Also, during difficult times, many company leaders would rather be surrounded by close, supportive acquaintances than distant strangers whose loyalty they're not really sure they can count on.

How do you get to know your boss better? Call up his secretary and make an appointment to see him. Try to schedule something early, really early, because your boss is less likely to be tied up then, and because it shows you're an employee who gets in early. If the secretary asks you what the appointment is about, tell him it's of a personal nature. Almost all company presidents will honor such a request for a meeting.

What do you talk about when you do get in to see her? Come prepared. Be frank. Tell her you don't feel you know her well enough and that you'd like to inform her of what you're up to. Give her a rundown on what you're working on and the status of this work. Tell her that you like working for the company very much, and that you'd like to help in any way possible. Your boss will appreciate your concern and interest. Very few employees have the confidence to be so bold and direct as to schedule such an appointment. If you do, it will quickly put you on the map with your boss.

Get to know his pace and style, too—and consider adjusting yours accordingly. An advertising agency executive told me about this incident: "My first boss once turned to me as I was lagging behind him while walking down the hall, and said, 'Do you want to keep up with me or not?' It had a symbolic as well as a literal meaning—it was a warning—and I never forgot it." The head of a law firm mentioned pace, too: "I like people who walk quickly. Generally there's a connection between how they think and work and how they walk."

It's also important not to let things lapse after you've made an initial attempt to get to know your boss better. Make it a point to stick your head in her office once a week or so, even if only to say hello. It'll give her a chance to ask how your various assignments and projects are going. If you pass him in the hall, mention—*briefly*—what you're currently doing. Once you get to know him a bit, you might invite him to your home for dinner. "I like it when ambitious employees approach me," said one executive. "I like to see employees in their homes and family environments—it's useful to me to know where their decisions are coming from." But make sure he's the type who welcomes this sort of invitation. Some bosses don't. ("Any invitations should come from above," said one.)

I must, of course, point out that certain bosses—and thank goodness, they are few and far between—are distant and standoffish. Often it's because they are shy or afraid to get too close to their employees. These people are almost impossible to get close to, and I wouldn't exert much energy or spend time trying to do so. You'll just annoy them.

Fortunately, this kind of company leader is very much in the minority, and the chances are your boss will be glad to get to know you better.

Chapter Twenty-five

Let Your Boss Know about the Great Work You're Doing

Don't just sit there and do good work. Tell your boss about it. Sure, he may find out about it from your direct superiors. He may hear about it through the grapevine. But it also may escape him completely. Bosses are busy people. Sometimes they may have responsibility for as many as several hundred employees, so occasionally it's difficult for them to get a fix on who's doing what. And the unfortunate truth is, bosses tend to find out much more quickly when you do a bad job than when you do a good job.

If you're doing exceptionally good work, make damn sure your boss knows about it. Right away. You don't want anyone else taking credit for it, and you also don't want your boss to overlook you—especially when you're contributing so much. How do you tell your boss you're doing a super job? Simple. You walk into her office and say, "Hi, Susan. I want to bring you up to date on such and such a project," or, "I want to tell you about the important meeting today on the new Jones account."

But be sure to have something to talk about—don't bother your boss just to pass the time of day. "You can make a pest of yourself unless you have concrete reasons for making your presence known," said an executive vice president. "The person you're trying to impress will see through you in a minute. But if you have something significant to say, a new method of operating in a certain area that's more efficient, any idea for better productivity, that's fine. Don't just mouth platitudes."

Your boss is a busy person. Don't waste her time. Let's say she asks you to write a report. When you go in to present it, don't have a handful of notes and scraps of paper. Organize yourself thoroughly first. Rehearse what you're going to say, and be prepared to defend your conclusions. Most important, hand her a clear, clean, thorough, finished product. And while you're preparing the report, don't drop into her office every half hour to tell her how you're doing. You're not a child anymore, and you don't need constant reassurance. Do a terrific job on the project, finish it a day early, and then present to the boss something you're really proud of.

One thirty-three-year-old company president I spoke to—an extremely dynamic, successful man—told me he started giving his boss progress reports the very first year he was with the company. He was good, he knew he was good, and he wanted the people above him to know about it as quickly and as directly as possible. And yet he didn't want to appear to be bragging. The way he got around that was by giving status reports on all the assignments he was working on. He realized his boss would naturally be interested in these reports because he would want to know what was going on in the company. And so it was a perfect situation for subtly and sometimes not so subtly letting his boss know not only the status of a particular assignment, but also how brilliantly he was executing it. Apparently his system worked well. He was made president of a forty-million-dollar shoe company at the age of thirty-one.

Chapter Twenty-six

Read a Trade Publication, or Several

Many company presidents told me they especially like it when they get the feeling that an employee really loves his job, not just for the money but for the satisfaction he gets from working for that particular company in that particular industry.

How can you show your boss that you take more than just a mild interest in the steel business, or the grocery business, or whatever business you happen to be in? Read a trade publication. Every week. Read half a dozen, in fact. In many ways, it's never been easier. These days, the vast majority of trade publications are online.

Now, I'm not suggesting you stroll by your boss's office, magazine in hand. Or try to station yourself in the bathroom stall next to his so you can discreetly place your copy of *Bottlers United* on the floor for him to see. That's not what I mean at all.

My point is this: If you read the trade publications in your particular industry, you'll learn more about your business— plenty more. And it'll be interesting. It'll give you ideas. You'll learn what the competition is up to, possibly get some new money-saving ideas, and maybe some money-making ones as well. All this will be reflected in your general conversation and in your attitude. In fact, you'll probably start to take a livelier interest in what you're doing. And do a better job at it.

"Many people in industry don't understand the workings of the industry or their competitors or even their own company," according to the executive vice president of a large securities firm. "Find out everything you can. Read, study, expose yourself to all the information you can find. What makes one firm different from another? Find out about the style of senior management in your company and competing companies. Come up with creative ideas and programs that will make your company stand out from its competitors. Ask yourself, 'How can I help my firm fit into the marketplace of the present?'"

Trade publications can make you a more interesting and valuable employee. So read them. Sooner or later, your boss will notice the difference. It's all part of becoming the indispensable employee.

Chapter Twenty-seven

Get into the Profit Arena

When times are good, staff jobs are important. But when money gets tight, they're often the first to go. Companies always need to keep their sales forces and production people because they contribute directly to the lifeblood of the company. Without them, no new cash would be coming in and no product could be shipped out. But people who are in charge of new product ideas or office furnishings or company public relations start to become very expendable.

The head of a small but highly profitable software company told me that he recently disbanded his entire research and development staff. Why? "Because during times like these, I'm just not bringing out any new products. My established line is selling reasonably well; it has all the kinks out of it, it throws off a good profit, so we're putting all our energy behind selling as much of it as possible. When times are flush I can afford to invest in the future. But now just isn't the time for it. It's too risky. I want to keep as much ready capital on hand as possible. You never know when you're going to need it."

Are you in a staff job? Is your specialty public relations? Creative thinking? Are you an "idea person"? A strategic planner? A futurist?

Then I suggest you begin today, wherever possible, to move yourself onto the line. The more you can become involved with generating new business, increasing sales, finding new customers and new markets, the more secure you're going to be when times get tough.

The one thing companies need now more than ever is to have money coming in. And the more you have to do with bringing that money in, the less expendable you're going to be. It's as simple and as basic as that. "If you can develop a profitable area of responsibility and make it grow at a rate faster than that of the industry," said one executive, "I guarantee you're going to be noticed by senior management."

I realize, of course, that there are millions of staff jobs, very important ones, all across the United States. And if you've been a staff person for twenty or thirty years, it's not very easy to jump into new areas and new departments. Well, if that's the case, I don't mean to alarm or panic you. I just urge you to keep your eyes wide open and ask yourself, *How important am I to the company, really? If they got rid of me and my whole department, would the company be able to survive? What are we actually contributing in the way of the daily intake of hard cash?*

If your answers to all these questions make you feel terribly uneasy, I suggest that you start thinking seriously about how you can help your company make more money—or at least save more money. Now. Even in your staff job. Put to work today some of those good long-range ideas you've had. It can be done. And if you can do it, you'll become an indispensable employee.

Chapter Twenty-eight

Cultivate Your Client Relationships

Do you deal directly with your company's clients? Are you a salesperson? A broker? A demonstrator?

Then cultivate your relationships with your clients—more than you ever have before. Call them on the phone, or call on them in person, more than you used to. Take them out to lunch. Send them a Christmas gift, something thoughtful and personal that says you've really come to know who they are. Send them a cute or clever e-card—it costs next to nothing, and if it's really funny or heartwarming, your client will really get a kick out of it.

You don't have to spend a lot of money, just show them you're interested. People, especially clients, appreciate lots and lots of attention. In fact, they love it. Not to the point where you bother them, or they begin to feel you're trying to get too close, but show a casual interest. Cool. Discreet.

Today many business people look upon a really close relationship with their clients as old-fashioned, outmoded. Well, it's not. Clients are, and will always be, the lifeblood of your company. And if you're important to and liked by your clients, your company will sense that—and not want to tamper with it. "The rapport a salesperson has with his clients is the most important asset he has," says a top executive. "One develops that rapport by always doing what's in the best interests of the customer—and thus also in the best interests of the firm."

One company president told me he would have fired one of his salesmen years ago. The guy hardly sold enough goods to cover his draw. But because he had such an incredibly close relationship with a dozen or so of his customers, his boss was afraid to fire him. He figured the salesman would go out and get a job with the competition and take his customers with him. And that would have cost a lot more money than keeping the salesman around. So that's what he did—he kept him around.

The moral of the story is this: Now is the time to spend more time and energy than ever before in servicing your clients. Sitting at your desk right now wondering what to do with yourself? Hop on your computer and e-mail a client you haven't been in contact with for a while. He or she may be happier to hear from you than you ever imagined. Maybe they're sitting around like a lot of people these days, worrying about their job. Maybe they'll enjoy schmoozing with you. Give it a shot—it's worth it.

Chapter Twenty-nine

Sell Harder

This is a particularly important chapter to those of you who are in sales, or who do some selling as part of your job. It has to do with how to be a better, more positive, more aggressive salesperson.

I interviewed the sales manager of a medium-sized food company, and he gave me some fascinating insights into what he's looking for in his sales force. "Due to the steep rise in the cost of several of our key ingredients," she said, "we've been raising our prices almost every month, and we've just got to pass these increases on if we're going to stay in business. But most of my sales force doesn't seem to understand that. All they do is bitch, as if we're the only ones raising prices. The fact is, everybody is raising prices in this kind of economy, and our customers half expect it.

"But that's little consolation to most of my sales force. All I hear from them is how difficult it is to sell our products, how we've got to give our customers more quality, more service, lower prices, bigger discounts. I ask myself, *Who are these guys working for—me or their customers?* I want them working for me 100 percent! Instead of walking into their accounts full of apologies and explanations and promises of deals to come, they ought to be going in full of confidence and belief in the products they're selling, no matter what they cost. The way to sell is to tell yourself, *I've got a great line of products—the very best!—and the price is fair. Now all I have to do is convince my customer of that. I'm going to go all out to excite him or her about the superior features of my products.*

What's the message in this? Simply that sales managers and company presidents are in no mood to hear about all your negative feelings. They know they've raised prices to the breaking point and may have to raise them even higher. They're not happy about it, but in order to stay in business, they've got to do it. So the last thing they want to hear from you is how impossible it is to sell at these prices. They know it's difficult. But that's what they've hired you for—to sell, not to complain. So stop complaining. It's not going to bring prices down, and it may actually bring your sales down.

Your customers will immediately pick up on your negative attitude.

You know in your heart that the best way to sell more than the next guy is to charge into your accounts and get them really fired up about what you're selling. If you can do that, they'll buy from you no matter what you're charging.

So give it a try. Keep your negative feelings under your hat and think of all the good things about the products you're selling. Then tell your customers about them. You'll not only be pleasing your boss, you'll be making lots of money on juicy commissions.

Chapter Thirty

Be a Great Communicator

No one would deny that it's tremendously important to be a good listener. In fact, according to the head partner of a large law firm, "You never learn anything when you're talking." Maybe *you* don't learn when you're talking—but other people are sure learning a lot about you. They're learning not only such elementary things as whether you have a pleasant-sounding voice and whether you use the language correctly, but also what sort of person you are, whether or not you have the potential for success, how confident you are, how well you can handle other people, and so on.

Most of the executives I talked to mentioned how important it is to be able to communicate effectively. Obviously, it can be a crucial factor in whether or not you get the job in the first place. Said one company president: "The decision to seriously consider someone for a job is usually made within ninety seconds. It's a question of how the prospect talks, listens, and 'sells' herself; a question of eye contact and body language; of how quick and responsive she seems to be. Most of our customers will be meeting our company by telephone only, so the way our employees communicate is tremendously important. There's a certain self-confidence, a certain sense of presence, that comes through in someone who's an effective communicator. I have a weakness for that type of person." Don't we all?

Of course, the ability to communicate well with clients is particularly important for people in sales. "A salesperson's greatest value lies in how well he or she can charm the customer into buying the product," said the CEO of a children's clothing company. But the value of communication doesn't stop there. Anyone who aims for the top has to "sell himself" every inch of the way. He has to get along with fellow employees: that's communication. He has to bring himself and his work to the notice of upper management: that's another kind of communication. He has to communicate to his superiors that he can handle more responsibility, that he has leadership potential. He has to communicate with the outside world as a representative of his company.

An executive I quoted earlier mentioned eye contact and body language: gestures, posture, how you sit or stand. They're all part of how you communicate. You can be terribly articulate and well-spoken and still create a very negative impression if you're shifty-eyed or you slump in your chair or you constantly engage in nervous gestures like picking at your clothes, touching your face, or wringing your hands. A shaky or too-soft voice, a cringing posture, tightly crossed arms and legs that suggest you're all closed in on yourself—these things reveal a lack of confidence that can spell failure to get a promotion or a raise, or even failure to keep your job.

Here's what an advertising company executive said of one of his creative directors: "Not only does she prepare a tremendously good product, but the way she presents herself makes you feel that she's an exciting, intelligent human being. You want to be around her."

If you aren't sure you convey that kind of impression—if you're sometimes a bit tongue-tied or at a loss for words, if you have trouble expressing your thoughts clearly, if talking in a business situation makes you stammer and sweat, or if people have complained that you speak too loudly or softly or fast or slow—take a course in effective communication.

You can practice on your own, too. Talk in front of the mirror and watch your body language. Does it reflect ease, confidence, poise without arrogance? Tape yourself. Does your voice have a pleasant pitch? Do you speak clearly and at a moderate pace? When you have something to say to the boss, practice first on a friend or a member of your family. In these ways, you'll learn how to present yourself and your ideas smoothly, clearly, articulately, and with confidence. Often, just the realization that speaking well and clearly is important is enough to spur you to present yourself in a better light.

Chapter Thirty-one

Looking Good Counts

Not too many years ago there was a movement in business, even in stodgy law firms and investment houses, to a more casual dress code. In advertising, the industry in which I came of age, account executives in many firms stopped wearing a jacket and a tie every day, only donning the uniform on those days they knew they were going to see a client. People in the creative departments really let their hair down, some wearing sandals, shorts, unkempt beards, torn jeans. I can tell you that even as a liberal, forward-thinking, ultramodern creative director, I could never quite get over how unbelievably sloppy some of the members of my department dressed. As they were presenting ideas to me, I would think, *Man, I would never let someone like this present to a client.* Because it was their right to dress this way, I never criticized their appearance. But I must confess, their slovenliness turned me off; and even if they were extremely talented, I would have had a really hard time promoting them to the next level.

I don't think there are any of us who would want to return to a time when men were expected to wear a suit and a tie every day, and women were required to wear a suit and high heels. But that doesn't mean we shouldn't look crisp and clean and well-shaven and coiffed on days we're going to the office.

The plain truth is that the human animal seems to prefer to be around people who are pleasant to look at rather than people who appear scruffy and dirty. The care you take with your appearance is often seen as an indication of what you think of yourself, of how much pride you take in your job and company. Company leaders don't want somebody who looks like a slob representing their corporation to the outside world. "We want our employees to have an appearance that's symbolic of our company's reputation," said the chairman of the board of a large metropolitan newspaper. "If they have any contact with the public and don't dress neatly and appropriately, it tarnishes the paper's image."

Your company probably has its own dress code. Certain

fields, like banking, tend to want their employees to dress conservatively; others, such as advertising, are more relaxed about dress requirements. But make no mistake: appearance matters to *every* company. Consider that companies willingly spends millions of dollars on the logo they choose to represent them before the public. Clearly, image is important. Studies have shown that employers consider well-dressed and well-groomed workers to be more intelligent and responsible than those who make a poor appearance. Keep that firmly in mind as you get dressed for work today.

Chapter Thirty-two

Take the Peer Test

Are you more indispensable than the person working in the very next office who has the very same job as you? To find out, ask yourself these questions: Who works harder? Who gets in earlier? Who takes a shorter lunch hour? Who stays later? Who takes work home? Who's closer with his or her immediate boss? The boss's boss? Ask yourself: Who knows more about the competition? The industry in general? The company itself? Who's more reliable? Who executes an assignment more professionally? More quickly?

In short, compare yourself to your neighbor on every possible level.

If there's any question in your mind that she might be

more indispensable than you are—even the tiniest bit—it's time to get to work, time to get in earlier, to stay later, to take work home with you, to start reading the trade publications, to do everything you can to make yourself a more valuable employee than your peer.

And you can do all this very systematically. Find out what time your coworker gets in each morning. If it's 8:45, get in at 8:30. If he reads two trade magazines, why don't you read four? If she takes three days to complete an assignment, see if you can get it done in two.

Now I don't mean to suggest that you should focus on the person in the next office to the exclusion of all else. That can be a huge mistake. Both of you could get fired—he because he's not particularly good, and you because you've decided to be just a little bit better. My point is that if people on your level are working harder and performing better, it's time to start pushing yourself.

"Peer comparison is very important," according to one top executive I interviewed. "When you sit next to someone who's really producing, it's essential to ask yourself, 'What's she doing that I'm not?' It gives you that extra push." These are times when employees have to give more of themselves; more, possibly, than they ever imagined giving. When the economy is depressed, it's little consolation to be doing a pretty good job when those around you are doing a great job.

Chapter Thirty-three

Turning Things Around

Several years ago, I gave a negative evaluation to a bright supervisor. Although I couldn't really fault his work, I was unhappy with his overall attitude. He never seemed to be around. He wasn't doing as much as I knew he could. Others complained about working with him. He complained about working with others. No one was good enough for him.

In short, I felt that the company wasn't getting a fair return on its investment in him. And I felt it important that he be informed of it.

I didn't look forward to confronting Arthur. He is masterful at manipulating and twisting another person's words so that nothing is resolved, no criticism taken. I was of half a mind just to fire him. A lot of other bosses wouldn't have thought twice.

As it turned out, he wouldn't let me. Having read my evaluation, he scheduled an appointment to discuss it. I resolved not to let him leave my office until we decided on some corrective action, even if it meant his looking for another job.

Arthur seemed equally resolved, yet before I knew it, he was manipulating my criticism. "Of course I leave early when I've completed an assignment. I'm good at what I do, unlike some of the other people around here. You don't want me just sitting around twiddling my thumbs, do you?"

"A lot of your coworkers have told me they don't want to work with you because they say you're abrasive," I told him.

"Of course they think I'm abrasive. That's because I'm direct. You don't want me wasting half a day just so that some poor hack's ego doesn't get bruised. That's the trouble with this place. Everybody's so polite."

So there we were, Arthur cleverly managing to talk himself and me out of my carefully thought-out evaluation. Finally, I just said, "Shut up, Arthur. You're too damn smart for your own good." He looked alarmed. "You're twisting the truth, and you're not hearing me. No matter how you want to see it, I'm not happy with your performance and you've got to do something about it."

"What can I do?"

"When you complete an assignment, find another one. Immediately."

"You never give me other assignments."

"That's because I can't always be monitoring your workload. You need to let me know when you need work. It's also difficult for me to find a partner for you—you don't like working with anyone. We work as teams here."

"There are some people I like working with."

Slowly, methodically, we worked out a list of people with whom Arthur felt he could connect. He agreed to load up on assignments. All the resistance, the manipulation, seemed to have gone out of him.

Over the next few months, every time a new assignment came up, I included Arthur among the teams of people working on it. He soon became a changed employee, working harder, producing far more, and interfacing with others with a whole new spirit. Before I knew it, I felt he was earning every penny of his salary, and then some. The company was getting its money's worth.

The moral of the story? Arthur made a vigorous effort to deal with a negative evaluation. He could have ignored it, hoping it would go away. But he chose to confront it head-on. Fortunately for him, I wouldn't let him talk me out of the criticisms. Then, once they had been identified, he dedicated himself to turning those negatives around.

You can do the same. If real negatives exist about you at your job, figure out exactly what they are (but don't go *seeking* criticism in this environment, whatever you do), work out a specific, tangible plan for turning them around, and then throw yourself into it for all you're worth.

Keep in mind that you're not simply making a good impression, you're *turning around* a negative one, which is much, much harder. It can be done, but it will take a dedication to your work you may never have had before.

Monitor your progress. Are you working 33 percent more hours? Arthur, for example, is. In fact, he has almost completely turned around my opinion of him.

Are you getting significantly more work done?

Is it of the highest possible quality?

Above all, don't quibble with your boss's criticism of you. Turn it around.

Chapter Thirty-four

Be Inventive

Here's one of the best ways I've ever heard of for making sure you keep your job in a tight economy. You read in a previous chapter about finding out what your company's problems are and then putting your mind to work solving them. Take this a step further. Identify a brand-new way to create efficiency or a new way for the company to make money, one nobody has ever thought of before. And don't be so sure you can't be good at it. After all, have you ever really thought about it before? Have you ever sat down and asked yourself, Is there a way this department could be run more efficiently? Are there any new assignments we could take on? Any new areas we could get into?

I don't personally know each and every business you might

be in, but I do know that just about any system can be stream-lined, and that departments can often easily take on related yet new and different functions. Here's an example one com-pany president told me about: "The woman we have at the switchboard wanted to get her files in order. She said to me, 'Get me a long cord for my headphones so I can walk ten or fifteen feet from the board and work on the files at the same time.' I thought that was fantastic. The cord was inexpensive, and she became much more productive. I like people who are always thinking, always doing."

So sit down and think about what your company does and how it does it. Is there any way to improve upon it? Write your ideas down. Discuss them with people on your own level whom you feel you can trust (after all, you don't want them taking credit for your good ideas). If any of the ideas seem to make good sense, take them to your immediate supervisor.

Smart companies welcome such suggestions. "Our em-ployees receive up to 10 percent of the amount saved by their suggestions," explained the CEO of a large packaged goods company. "We're a profit-sharing company, so our employees know that the more they can save the company, the more they benefit. We have machinists who have invented tools that have simplified our production process. An art director just came up with a suggestion that will save five thousand dollars. Secretaries come up with ideas to save on postage, stationery, copying. Our vice chairman's assistant has had two suggestions approved and been rewarded for them. Our truck drivers are involved in designing the trucks so they're happy with them, take better care of them, and the trucks last longer."

One of my very best golfing buddies put himself on the map big-time in his early twenties with some truly inventive—but amazingly simple—thinking. He was working for one of our country's three biggest retailers at the time, a company that sold some fifteen million children's dresses a year. My friend noticed that all the dresses hung on hangers that carried their manufacturer's name—not the name of the retailer. He went in to his boss and said, "Why on earth are we giving free ad space to our suppliers when every one of those hangers could have our name on it?" His boss thought about it for a few seconds, then said, "What a great idea! Let's do it. Let's make all our suppliers hang the dresses they sell us on *our* hangers. Starting today. Make it happen." And just like that my friend, who was twenty-three at the time, was given the assignment of changing the hangers that fifteen million little girls' dresses hang on. In short, he became the giant retailer's newest and brightest shining star. It heralded the beginning of a truly meteoric career.

Even if your ideas prove to be unworkable, your superiors will appreciate the effort, and they'll be delighted that you take such an interest in the health and well-being of your company.

Chapter Thirty-five

Be Talented

Many people think that you are either born talented in a given area or you're not; and if you're not, there isn't much you can do about it.

Well, every CEO I spoke with totally disagreed with the above sentiment. In fact, they were almost vehement in their reaction against it.

One chief executive told me that he himself had failed miserably when he first began to work as a salesman. He was shy, quiet, introverted—everything a salesman isn't supposed to be. Did he give up and switch to another field? Not on your life. He made up his mind that he was going to become an expert at selling and devoted the next five years of his life to that very task. He read books on selling, he took courses on selling, he practiced in front of the mirror, he asked his prospective clients for comments on what he was doing wrong, he asked his sales manager for pointers. In fact, he did nothing but eat, sleep, and breathe salesmanship twenty-four hours a day. Despite the fact that he originally seemed to have no native talent for selling, he became a superior sales-man. And this was the platform on which his subsequent success was based.

Soon he became the leading salesperson in his corpora-tion. Before long he was made regional sales manager; the next year, national sales manager. Eventually he became the chief officer of his company.

Most of the successful businesspeople I interviewed told me that if a person works hard enough, throws himself into the job completely, and starts to believe in himself, he can become an expert at just about anything he wants.

"The gift of talent," said the president of an import com-pany, "is efficiency, motivation, and willingness to take on a lot of responsibility. You can be in administration, produc-tion, sales, any field—talent means dispensing all your du-ties in an extremely efficient way and then some. You know what's going on; you're very good at recognizing priorities; you don't waste time on trivia but tackle immediate prob-lems. You're not frightened of responsibility. You know how to delegate work. You can work with other people and inspire them to work hard."

Do you sometimes feel that you don't have enough inborn talent for whatever job you're doing? Well, don't worry about it. It doesn't matter whether you do or don't. Very few talented people are born that way. Most of them get there through hard work and dedication. And you can, too.

Chapter Thirty-six

Crossword Puzzle as Metaphor for Problem Solving

Okay, maybe you stink at crossword puzzles, or have absolutely zero interest in them. That's cool. Me, I love 'em. I do the *New York Times* puzzles Wednesday through Saturday. They get harder every day. Monday's is easy, Tuesday's is a little harder, Wednesday's is a bit of a challenge, and Friday's and Saturday's are absolute bears. Sunday's, which everybody thinks is the hardest, is actually at about Thursday's degree of difficulty—it's just a lot bigger.

Often, when I first glance at Saturday's puzzle, it seems as if I can barely fill in three to four words. So what I do is I keep the Saturday puzzle around the whole day—spend fifteen minutes with it over lunch, pick it up in the afternoon while watching a football game, try to get a couple of words when doing my stint on the treadmill. By and by, I find that what at first felt like an impossible task is slowly beginning to give way. I make an unexpected connection here; dredge up a word from the deepest corner of my cortex there; remember, some-how, the French word for window I learned as a high school sophomore. I spend a few minutes on the puzzle before I go to bed at night, and bring it into the loo with me on Sunday morning. And most weekends, by the time Sunday afternoon rolls around, I've completed Saturday's puzzle.

In truth, I never expected to finish it. But some thirty-six hours or so later, despite a powerful feeling of pessimism, I've solved it.

Now what on earth does this have to do with your job? With becoming an indispensable employee?

Two things. First, most people at some time—or maybe frequently—get an assignment that is difficult and amor-phous. For example, when I was in advertising, it could have been something like: Come up with a brilliant new ad cam-paign for Kraft mayonnaise. *A brilliant ad for a mayonnaise that's been around for close to a century?* How the hell do you do that?

Well, just like with Saturday's crossword puzzle, I would bring home my assignment sheet, along with my first lame attempts at a clever campaign, and keep them by my side for the evening. I'd go over them while I was on the exercise bike. Glance at them while I was watching the news. Read through them once more on the can. And, of course, spend a few more minutes with my notes before I turned out the light for the evening. And if I'd wake up in the middle of the night and couldn't get back to sleep for a while, I'd go over them yet again, scribbling down any new thoughts and ideas that popped into mind, no matter how crazy, no matter how lame.

Now, I'm not saying it worked every time, but I can tell you this: I came up with some of my very best ad campaigns—ones that garnered me raises, bonuses, promotions, and notoriety—in that very manner; by sticking with something that at first glance seemed damn near impossible. It's astonishing how a few extra minutes of concentration applied here and there can yield the most powerful results, the most brilliant breakthroughs. I'm not saying you should pour a dozen hours straight into work you bring home with you. All I'm suggesting is that you keep your assignment and your initial thoughts, doodles, and scratchings *nearby*, within reach, and pay them a little extra attention when you're in the mood, when it's convenient.

Just like with the crossword puzzle, you'll discover that by not giving up—even in the face of a powerful feeling of pessimism—you will, in fact, come up with ideas and solutions that are often brighter, stronger, more creative and valuable than you ever dreamed possible. Man, an employee who can do that soon becomes completely indispensable.

Crossword puzzle metaphor? One, don't give up. Keep the problem/assignment nearby to work on at intervals. You'll often solve something you thought was impossible.

Two, and perhaps more importantly, when you keep on plugging, even when feeling pessimistic and defeated, as if it's hopeless, you *succeed*! Isn't that amazing? You can use it as a life lesson again and again.

Chapter Thirty-seven

Be in the Right Place at the Right Time

Nearly every executive I interviewed for this book spoke modestly of having been lucky, of having been "in the right place at the right time." But when I asked for details, it turned out that it really wasn't a simple matter of luck. As one securities company executive put it, "You have to make your own luck, your own momentum."

In business, what we call "luck" is really a sort of sixth sense of where the action is (or where it's going to be). It's a matter of vision and imagination on a solid foundation of knowledge, and of a willingness to stick your neck out and take a risk.

How do you get that sixth sense, that vision? It's easy for me to say "Make your own luck." But *how* do you do it?

You begin by knowing what you want, what you're aiming for, and you keep that in mind at all times: while you're learning all you can about what your company and its competitors do; while you're thinking about how it can be done better; while you're putting forward ideas.

Remember that you're never "stuck" unless you want to be. If your area of the company doesn't seem to be going anywhere, *you can move*. If a task force is organized to develop a project that seems to have real potential for success, *ask to be included*, even if you weren't originally picked—you'll impress people with your eagerness. As I've stressed throughout this book, corporate management values nothing if not gumption and drive.

How can you tell if a project has potential or not? The answer has a lot to do with instinct, with that sixth sense I mentioned before. But it's not 100 percent instinctive by any means. There is a way to develop one's ability to spot critical new projects: Step back occasionally and take an overview of what's going on in your company. Is it seeking a major new piece of business? Bringing out a product that may open a whole new stream of investors and speculators? Exploring a related field or possible fertile territory for new growth? Do all your homework—reading, keeping your eyes and ears open, staying up to date on the Internet, earmarking any and all websites that relate to your company and its line of business—so you can make educated guesses as to whether or not any of these new ventures will bear fruit. And then, if you have a hunch one will, do your damnedest to get involved.

Be flexible. Remember that you may not be able to achieve all of your goals at once, and that you may have to make some temporary sacrifices in the interest of long-term gains. For instance, if being in the right place at the right time means you have to move from one part of the country to another, then you must be willing to do it (and let management know that you are). If you're going to move within your company from, say, sales into management, you must realize that a very successful salesman usually makes more money than a manager, so you may have to take a salary cut for the time being. "What might not be in your short-term interests might be in your best long-term interests," said the new president of an investment firm.

Be on the alert for those opportunities—in an active, dynamic company they come up more frequently than you might think—to make yourself and your accomplishments visible. Maybe your boss asks a coworker to prepare a report, but the coworker's too busy. Go in and ask the boss if you can do the assignment. Or you learn that your company is pitching a clothing account. Three years ago you worked on that very account when you were with another company, and you know the inside story on the company—their problems, their needs. Don't keep it to yourself. Draw up a report on the company and present it to your boss.

Keep tabs on the grapevine for information about the company's health and prospects and about positions that may be opening due to promotions. Secretaries and assistants often learn of hot news well before everybody. Is the company changing its direction, and will it therefore be looking for new people and skills? Is it in a temporary slump—or a permanent one?

Making your own luck—being in the right place at the right time—means looking beyond today or this week or this year. It means choosing the tremendously promising, if slightly risky, venture over the safe and predictable path. It means thinking creatively. And it means being assertive—remembering always that your destiny is in your own hands.

Chapter Thirty-eight

Think New Products

One of my best friends in the world just so happens to be the single greatest business person I've ever known. Lew Frankfort is the CEO of Coach, the upscale makers of great leatherware fashions. In 1985, Coach sales were about nineteen million dollars. In 2008, Coach sales were over two billion dollars! Way to go, Lew!

There are dozens of reasons why Lew is so successful—he works long days, pays his employees well, finds excellent people, insists on excellence throughout the entire company. I could go on and on—I really could. But one particular piece of Frankfortian advice stands out for me above all others. Coach has grown so spectacularly because of Lew's insistence that it bring out *new* products every season. Lew's thinking is that you need to keep giving people new reasons to come into your store, to visit you online, to leaf through your catalog.

And that is precisely why, in this difficult economic environment, I urge you to think "New Product." Now more than ever, no matter what business you're in, you need to give your customer a new reason to look at you. Customers are more reluctant to spend money than ever before. Dollars are tight. Credit is tight. And to top it all off, there is a mood afoot, even among the very rich, that unnecessary spending is somehow decadent. *Why buy a new car or refrigerator or pair of shoes now when the ones I have are still good? Better to save my money in case I get fired.*

Given this mind-set, why would anyone ever want to look at your product line except by happenstance? After all, if your product line isn't changing, your customer is well aware of it. It's *familiar*. There's nothing new or innovative or sexy about it.

That's why I heartily encourage you—particularly if you're in research and development, new product design, sales, or promotion—to think of new additions to your product line. Which of your products could use an upgrade? It doesn't have to be a huge change—after all, in this climate, few companies have the resources to pour millions of dollars into new and improved products. But sometimes creative, out-of-the-box thinking can lead to a simple but brilliant little change in a product that the marketplace has been yearning for. At the very least, the improvement can be something that advertising and promotion can create a little hoopla behind, enough to get people to look at your product again.

I ran a publishing company for many years and one of our mainstay books, *How To Pick Up Girls*, was running out of gas. My tireless assistant suggested we do a pocket-sized version of the book for guys to carry when they went to singles bars, a version small enough to keep in their back pocket, chock-full of the book's more important tips but unobtrusive enough that a guy could duck into the men's room and brush up on his technique. The pocket-sized book had nothing in it that wasn't in the original edition, it was just smaller and cheaper to produce. But it wound up generating tons of new sales and, more importantly, got people to take a second look at our entire line.

My experience in business is that if you want people to form a strong and energized relationship with your brand, you've got to keep on exciting them about your brand with new colors, shapes, product improvements—new *news*!

So get to it—what small but surprising twist can you think up to add new, exciting life to your company's product line? You don't have to come up with something overnight. Just let your mind wander to the subject for fifteen minutes here, a half hour there, skip a day, and then think about it over morning coffee. Discuss it with your significant other, or a friend in another line of work. You'll surprise yourself with your creativity.

Then, when you have an idea that excites you, that you really think can work, lay it on your boss. Even if she doesn't like the idea, she'll be blown away by your interest, your dedication to the well-being of your firm. Stoke her up on the importance of coming up with something new. Be a champion of it. You'll probably get *her* thinking about a product improvement. You may even wind up brainstorming together— not a bad way of securing your job!

Chapter Thirty-nine

Make Sure You Work for a Fine Company

By the time you've absorbed all the advice in this book, you'll be prepared to be a highly valued member of any corporate team. Here's something to think about: Is the corporate team you're on—or thinking of getting on—one that's worthy of your talents and dedication?

Think about all the time and energy you spent deciding which college to attend. It was an important decision, one that would have an effect on your whole future—and you gave it the attention it deserved. And what about choosing a career? Didn't you think long and hard before you determined the work you wanted to spend most of your adult life doing? Well, choosing the environment in which you're going to do that work is an equally important decision, and not one to be made lightly. Think about it: You're going to be spending the majority of your waking hours at work, going to and from work, getting ready for work, thinking about work, and reading and studying so you can do a better job. Isn't it worth taking some time out now to find the best possible company?

When you've got several companies in mind, ask around. Talk to people who work at them. By asking a lot of questions of a lot of people, you can get a fix on the company's reputation pretty quickly: Is it an up-and-coming corporation with an eye on the future and plenty of room for growth? Does it offer substantial rewards to dedicated, hard-working employees? Does it maintain a reasonable, friendly atmosphere, or is it run on the terror system? Are financial and other incentives so meager that the employees' philosophy is "Do as little as you can get away with"? Is management stuck in outdated ways of thinking and doing things? Do you notice a great many sons, cousins, and daughters-in-law of the owners being hired?

"Our company's most important asset is good teamwork," said the general manager of a large electronics firm. "We try to have the best possible communication between supervisors and employees, because if we all know each other well, we can work that much better. We are willing to make allowances for personal problems—maybe someone has to leave a little early once in a while—as long as our people work hard and are also willing to do that little bit extra. We make sure each employee knows we really value her and need her help. We help them with their education, we encourage them and ask them to grow along with the company."

Now that's the kind of company philosophy to look for.

Don't settle for a company that allows its employees to idle through their days. "If you're really smart," said another top executive, "you'll get into a company that is demanding, that evaluates you regularly, that tells you what it expects of you and is really candid with you. Most companies didn't do this twenty or thirty years ago. If you didn't measure up, they'd just let you go. Now, we stay very close to our people. We want them to succeed, because if they succeed, that means we're going to be successful. Our number one goal over the next decade is the recruiting and training of good people."

If you take the time and the trouble to pick a good company, good things will happen to you. And if you're presently working for a company whose values and practices leave a lot to be desired, then perhaps it's time to start looking for a new job. The fact is, it's very unlikely that the company is going to change. A bad company is usually a bad company forever. And you don't want to have all the time, talent, and energy you're putting into it to wind up counting for naught.

Chapter Forty

Talk Things Over With Your Spouse/Partner/Family

Here is an idea I feel absolutely passionate about: Many of us who work in high-pressure jobs, especially in an economy like this, can feel isolated and alone. The pressures of work often keep us from talking with our colleagues on anything but the most superficial level. And when we get home we're so tired, irritable, or depressed about a tough, and maybe even defeating, day, that we don't discuss our jobs with our husbands, wives, partners, children.

And that can be a terrible mistake for a number of reasons.

First of all, it's not good to let things fester inside you. Talk them out. You'll feel better. Even if at first it seems like too much hard work, you'll soon see that it gives you a great feeling of release. Problems that seemed insurmountable will suddenly look manageable. They won't weigh so heavily on your mind, and you'll be able to enjoy your dinner and your evening a lot more.

Secondly, talking about your problems will help relieve that terribly isolated feeling. If the people you're closest to know what you're up against, they will be vastly more understanding of what you're going through.

Thirdly, you were probably first attracted to your partner/ husband/wife because you thought he or she was smart and had good judgment. Well, take advantage of those smarts. Get their insight and point of view. It may be far more illuminating and helpful than you ever dreamed it could be. Your significant other's distance from your situation may allow him or her to have a more objective, unclouded view of things; he or she may very well come up with some solutions that totally escaped you and that will make you look very good at the office.

And finally, during tough times like these, you're probably going to be spending more time at the office than ever before. If you describe the difficulties of your job to your spouse/ partner, he or she will better understand why it's necessary for you to spend so much time away from home and family. Significant others can start to feel rejected and resentful when their partner is spending 70 to 80 percent of his or her waking life at the office. And those feelings aren't good for partnerships or marriages or kids or anybody.

So let your spouse/partner know why you've got to work so hard and so long. It will make him or her feel more positive about the whole situation. That way there will be less pressure on you at home, and you'll be able to function at work with a clearer, less cluttered mind.

Chapter Forty-one

Become Irreplaceable

Here is the most surefire method there is for becoming an indispensable employee: Master your particular function so completely, so totally, so absolutely flawlessly, that your employer knows that if he were to let you go, he'd need two or even three people to replace you. Company president after company president told me that this is the best way he or she can think of for an employee to become indispensable.

And this isn't just a dream or a fantasy. Four or five of the presidents I talked with told me they actually have several men and women like this working for them right now. "I can think of one or two people," said a securities company executive, "whose expertise is absolutely critical to the bottom line of the firm."

The manager of a large fashion company told me about his fear that if he suddenly lost his office manager, his whole company would go to pieces. His office manager is a woman in her late thirties who has been with the company twelve years. She knows every one of his salespeople and all of their important clients. She knows the price structure better than he does, knows which of his clients is a good credit risk and which isn't, knows which salespeople fudge their expense accounts and which don't. In short, she is a sort of walking computer and encyclopedia of all there is to know about the internal workings of the entire company's sales, product, and pricing structure. If she were to leave, it would take at least two full-time people to replace her—and even then there would be untold chaos for six months to a year.

Do you want to become indispensable? Irreplaceable? Of course you do! Then get started. Learn as much about your job as you possibly can. And then learn even more. And after you do that, learn about related departments and how they interface with yours. "Just knowing your own area isn't enough," said one top executive. "If that's all you know about, you'll never advance beyond the niche you're in. You must continually broaden your horizons."

Of course, one of the most obvious areas in which to broaden your horizon is—I'm sure you've guessed it—computers. From the machines themselves to their myriad applications, business is ever more dependent on the world of computers. From Photoshop to Excel to PowerPoint, is there a business or a field of business in which our reliance on information technology isn't monumental?

I'm sure you know someone in your IT department who is indispensable to your company. Have you ever thought, *Wouldn't I like to be in her shoes?* Well, why not? I'm not suggesting that you quit art direction, or sales, or investment analysis, or whatever you do. But how about taking a computer course? My wife just bought a laptop that came with fifty hours of instruction for two dollars an hour. Imagine the leg up that could give you in your company. Let's face it, a great percentage of bosses, being in their late forties and older, are fairly computer illiterate. They're instantly impressed with employees who can help them navigate this whole new digital world.

I have an assistant who has put all my bill paying and frequent flyer information and bank activity online. I'd have to be put into a sanitarium if he left.

I know we all think about taking a course or two to gain genuine mastery of computer skills. But how many of you actually go ahead and do it? I can assure you, those who do are taking a giant step toward indispensability.

Chapter Forty-two

Just Keep Going

There seems to be a popular notion in America that in order to succeed you have to be supremely confident. You have to feel great about yourself. You have to "love" yourself. *Nonsense!* In my opinion, there is no more destructive idea in popular psychology than the one that decrees you have to feel 100 percent right about what you're doing, that you must feel positively positive about your abilities, your ideas, your approach.

Just about every self-help book I've ever read starts off placing a heavy, if not impossible, burden on the reader: Before you can expect to be successful at an undertaking, you must first learn to love yourself. I couldn't disagree more. Many of the most successful people I know are racked with self-doubt; they have a lack of confidence in their methods or ideas. Their strength is in their ability to move ahead no matter what their internal feelings. In fact, many will insist that it's their very self-doubt that propels them to work extra hard.

I have a simple motto: *Just keep going.* I can't tell you how many times I've left a client's office or bad meeting, or sat through a presentation that wasn't going well, and been tempted to pack it all in. To not show up at work the next day. To turn the assignment over to someone else. To start looking for a job somewhere else. To switch careers.

And yet, I never have. Long experience has taught me that most of the time we are our own most severe critics. We have a bad meeting and view it as a disaster. Meanwhile, our client and/or employer simply views it as a mild downward blip, just a single episode that is part of a long series of blips—some up, some down, but all generally part of a trend that is positive, profitable, the mark of a valuable employee.

It is those with the wisdom not to panic who endure. Some have a sudden success and try to milk it for all it's worth. Others experience failure and go to pieces. Neither reaction is warranted. Remember: Just keep going. History tells us this, religion tells us, our parents and coaches tell us, because it's true. If we don't give up, that which seems bleak, forbidding, and impossible today will tomorrow or the next day suddenly appear benign and conquerable. Indispensable employees know one thing for sure: They just keep going!

Chapter Forty-three

The Five Ways to Become an Indispensable Employee

I think you'll discover there are basically five different kinds of advice in this book, and I'd like to go over them once more in as simple and easy-to-master form as possible.

The first kind of advice is concerned with your attitude toward your job. If you're presently walking around with a chip on your shoulder, as if your company owes you a living, get rid of it. Nothing is more offensive to upper management, especially at a time like this. Instead of asking what your company can do for you, ask what you can do for your company. It will be greatly appreciated.

The second kind of advice is practical. Get in early, eat lunch at your desk, stay late, finish assignments on time (or even early). Little things like this all add up and can make a great impression.

The third kind of advice is inspirational. Go beyond yourself. Recognize and help solve your company's problems. Be creative, inventive; get into the profit arena. Just keep going.

The fourth kind of advice is political. Get to know your boss better. Let him know what you're up to. It's harder to get rid of someone you know well than someone who's almost a total stranger.

And the fifth kind of advice relates to your family. Talk things over with your spouse or partner or kids. During times like these you need sympathy and understanding. And who knows, someone who loves you, someone who's close to you, may just have the perspective to help you come up with an idea that'll make you a hero at the office.

In conclusion, I'd like to offer a little hope and optimism. I have a lot of faith in the American economy. We've been through recessions and depressions before, and we've always made it through with courage and character. Americans are hardworking and practical. We love business and free enterprise. Even with our economy in a real trough, the dollar is gaining strength against other currencies. Amazing, isn't it? When the world economy suffers, it's the United States that is seen as having the strongest financial foundation of all. This system has worked for us since 1776, and I feel confident it will work for us for a thousand years to come.

Granted, things look a little bleak sometimes, but before long our economy will be back on its feet and booming again. So take heart. You'll get through any tough time with flying colors. Just roll up your sleeves, let your company know you're willing to work as hard as you have to, and watch how quickly you become an indispensable employee.

Chapter Forty-four

A Tale of Two Employees

Before you march back out into the business world, ready to take your company by storm, I want you to take a little test. I'm going to describe for you a true-life incident involving two people. As you read about it I want you to ask yourself, as honestly as you can, which of the two you are most like.

A few years back, a young fellow named Hank worked as my assistant in my company, the Tenafly Film Company. One of our films, *Second Best*, was selected to be in the Sundance Film Festival. I told Hank he would have to come out to Sundance and help put up posters, make sure the prints of our film were in the right place at the right time, et cetera.

He asked if he could bring his girlfriend, Alyssa, along. She would fly out on the frequent flier points he'd accumulated, sleep in his hotel room, and even help with putting up posters. I said it was fine.

If you've never been to Sundance, let me tell you—it's a zoo. Every filmmaker and his or her friends run around like maniacs plastering every square inch of Park City with posters, banners, flyers, and promotional pieces. I did the same, with the help of my crew of four kids, my wife, my lawyer, Hank, and Alyssa. Every morning we'd meet in my rented condo at nine a.m. to plan our strategy for the day. Just before each meeting, Hank would sidle up to me and ask me if it was okay if he and Alyssa cut out early to go skiing. It would anger me, but I'd usually say yes because I figured Alyssa was out here on her own nickel and I was getting a free half-day's work out of her.

Then our meeting would begin, with everybody throwing around ideas about how best to get our posters up. And I couldn't help but notice what a willing participant Alyssa was in the discussion. She had great ideas. She volunteered to do the boldest, ballsiest poster placement. Meanwhile, Hank was sitting there, staring into space, his body language telling me that he just couldn't wait to get out of there and onto the slopes. *Wow,* I thought, *this dude who is being paid by me is nonchalanting his way through his work, and his lady friend, who doesn't owe me a thing, is getting caught up in the fun and spirit of making my film stand out at Sundance.* And that's how it went the entire week—Hank doing the bare minimum with a frown, and Alyssa throwing herself into the project as if it were her own.

Question? Who are you at your job? Hank or Alyssa? If you're Alyssa, you're going to do *great*! If you're Hank, think about it. What do you have to do to turn things around?

I know you can do it, Hank. You just need a little attitude adjustment. Go get 'em!